D0880549

TAKE FIVE

MEDITATIONS WITH JOHN HENRY NEWMAN

TAKE FIVE

MEDITATIONS WITH JOHN HENRY NEWMAN

MIKE AQUILINA & FR. JUAN R. VÉLEZ

Our Sunday Visitor Publishing Division
Our Sunday Visitor, Inc.
Huntington, Indiana 46750

Nihil Obstat
Msgr. Michael Heintz, Ph.D.
Censor Librorum

Imprimatur
✠ Kevin C. Rhoades
Bishop of Fort Wayne-South Bend
June 25, 2010

The Scripture citations used in this work are taken from the *Catholic Edition of the Revised Standard Version of the Bible* (RSV), copyright © 1965 and 1966 by the Division of Christian Education of the National Council of the Churches of Christ in the United States of America. Used by permission. All rights reserved.

Every reasonable effort has been made to determine copyright holders of excerpted materials and to secure permissions as needed. If any copyrighted materials have been inadvertently used in this work without proper credit being given in one form or another, please notify Our Sunday Visitor in writing so that future printings of this work may be corrected accordingly.

ISBN: 978-1-59276-800-4 (Inventory No. T1105)
LCCN: 2010929591

Cover design: Lindsey Riesen. **Cover art:** Portrait of Cardinal Newman (1801-90) (oil on canvas) by Sir John Everett Millais (1829-96), National Portrait Gallery, London, UK/The Bridgeman Art Library. **Interior layout:** Siok-Tin Sodbinow.

PRINTED IN THE UNITED STATES OF AMERICA

With filial gratitude, to our beloved
Pope Benedict XVI, who will beatify
Venerable John Henry Newman in
September, on the joyful commemoration
of the fifth anniversary year of his election
as successor of St. Peter

Contents

Acknowledgments

In this book, we have drawn (with some minor modifications from the original British style of spelling and punctuation) from the "uniform edition" of Newman's works, which was prepared by the cardinal himself late in his life. It was reprinted in its entirety in the first decade of the twentieth century. We would like to thank the institutions that have made these volumes available to us, especially the library of the University of California at Los Angeles.

Readers who wish to read our selections in context will find the complete works of Newman online at *http://NewmanReader.org*, which is maintained by the National Institute of Newman Studies (NINS). Readers who are especially grateful for Newman's insights should consider making a donation to NINS, which is a nonprofit research establishment. For those who want to go further in their encounter with Newman, we recommend *The Rule of Our Warfare: John Henry Newman and the True Christian Life*, compiled and edited by John Hulsman (Scepter Publishers, 2003).

We would like to thank the staff of Our Sunday Visitor for their encouragement in writing this book. In particular we wish to thank Bert Ghezzi and George Foster for their revision of the text.

MIKE AQUILINA
FR. JUAN R. VÉLEZ

How to Use This Book

Most Christians spend a large part of their waking hours in activity related to their work. They put in long shifts — on the shop floor, in the classroom, in the office, or at home with family responsibilities — and some spend additional time commuting to and from their labors. Thus, when they pass from this life, they will likely be judged to a great extent on what they did for a living.

Yet so many sermons and books on the spiritual life seem to ignore these everyday realities and focus instead on matters that are important — methods of meditation, volunteer work, almsgiving — but that hold a marginal place in the ordinary days of ordinary people.

In this book, we bring the rich teachings of Cardinal John Henry Newman to bear on the everyday circumstances of working life. Cardinal Newman lived a busy life as a teacher, editor, administrator, and clergyman — and he still found time enough to write books that have been profoundly influential in the fields of theology, philosophy, history, and fiction. His collected works fill dozens of volumes.

He was as busy a professional as you're likely to meet (or likely to become). Yet he was able to see the supernatural dimension of his tasks, even when they were mundane, difficult, or demanding of his entire attention.

How was Newman able to stay focused? He found very practical ways to bring Christ into the workday, and he shared some of his methods with us through his books, sermons, letters, and his interviews. He wrote about the importance of diplomacy in the workplace; about honesty; about dealing with disappointments and losing friends; about getting along with co-workers; and about the challenge of keeping one's eye on the goal, which is not worldly success, but godly glory. These spiritual counsels make up the bulk of this book's meditations.

Even if we never reach Cardinal Newman's level of prestige or production, we can still achieve the (more important) spiritual goals that God has set for our work. This is what God wants — and God is all-powerful — so he will give us all we need to succeed.

The best way to learn from Cardinal Newman is to get to know him first as a person and a teacher. Please begin by reading the brief outline of his life and summary of his contributions.

The meditations may be read in any sequence that suits you. They do follow a certain logic, moving from elementary to ultimate matters. But you may find it occasionally useful to jump around in search of the subject that occupies your mind.

Each meditation begins with an excerpt from Cardinal Newman's writings or teachings.

The meditation proceeds to a section titled "**Think About It**." There are a few points listed for you to consider in your prayer. You may refer them to yourself in God's presence, or refer them to God for answers, or both. Take time with each point. Don't rush. Wait quietly and patiently for God's response in your soul. He will not fail you — though his response may not be immediately sensible to you. Sometimes many years go by before we can see how God worked in our soul in prayer at a given moment.

Next is a section called "**Just Imagine**." A brief passage from Scripture is provided. Cardinal Newman's prayer and doctrine flow from a vivid, prayerful experience of the Scriptures. Try to enter these biblical scenes as a participant or an onlooker, so that you can personally experience the touch of Jesus, the teaching of Paul, and so on. Use your imagination!

Finally, you'll see a brief line or two with the heading "**Remember**." Copy this line onto a piece of paper and take it with you to work or post it on your refrigerator. Read it occasionally and repeat it as a prayer. See if you can pray it from memory by the end of the day.

Try to build time into your schedule so that you can pray one meditation — or pray without these meditations — for at least twenty minutes a day, preferably in the morning. Our relationship with God, like any personal relationship, grows deeper through conversation: intimate, heart-to-heart conversation. Workaholics look upon conversation as a luxury, but they're wrong. It is as necessary as drawing breath. It makes us human. And when our conversation is prayer, it makes us divine.

Try not to start your day without your morning prayer.

The Life of John Henry Newman

John Henry Newman was the most important English convert to Roman Catholicism in the nineteenth century — inspiring many other men and women to follow him to the fullness of faith — and he was one of the leading English writers of his time. He was a devoted son, brother, friend, scholar, writer, professor, and eventually, Catholic priest. His witness continues to influence people today who are inspired by his exemplary life of holiness.

John Henry Newman was born in the heart of the old city of London on February 21, 1801. He was the oldest of six children born to John Newman and Jemima Fourdrinier, an upper-middle-class family. Newman was educated at a private boarding school in Ealing, where he began his study of Latin and Greek. He did well in school and took up playing the violin and acting. He was raised in a devout Christian home in the "Low" Anglican Church Tradition. At home, the Bible was read and prayers were recited every day. While he was still in school, his father's banking business failed, and young Newman suffered poor health. Besides his struggles with health, Newman was also adversely affected by reading authors who questioned the Christian faith. This resulted in a brief distancing from religious practice; however, through the influence of Walter Mayers, a devout Calvinist clergyman, Newman had a religious conversion. He developed a vivid sense of God's presence in the world and of the reality of an invisible world that surrounds the visible world.

At the age of sixteen, Newman continued his studies at Trinity College, Oxford. There he worked hard and excelled. After completion of undergraduate work, he won a scholarship to continue his studies at Oxford and soon afterward he was elected a fellow of the prestigious Oriel College. At Oriel, Newman met intellectuals who questioned his Evangelical mindset. Newman began to discover the problems with Evangelical Anglicanism, and eventually this questioning led him to embrace the sacramental and ecclesiastical views of the "High Church" Anglicans.

As he was developing a deeper understanding of the sacraments and Tradition in Christianity, Newman began to teach at Oriel, where he had become a tutor. From the onset, he had the idea that a tutor should form the students assigned to him in virtue and religious practice. He thought that a tutor should be more than an academic instructor for undergraduates. Edward Hawkins, the provost at Oriel College, opposed Newman's ideas. Hawkins did not want Newman to change things. Eventually, Hawkins stopped assigning students to Newman and, in effect, forced Newman to retire, although Newman remained a fellow at Oriel.

When he stopped teaching at Oriel, Newman accompanied his friend Richard Hurrell Froude on a voyage in the Mediterranean; Froude was recovering from pulmonary tuberculosis. The trip was prolonged for six months, with two long stays: one in Rome and one in Sicily. In the latter, Newman came down with a sickness and was gravely ill for several weeks. The experience left him with a strong sense of a mission to accomplish; he felt that God had a plan for him in England. After recovering, Newman returned to England and within a week of his return, together with Froude, John Keble, and a few others, he launched a renewal movement. The movement soon came to be known as the Oxford Movement.

The Oxford reformers were well-educated Oxford graduates who wished to revive orthodox doctrine, sacramental practices, and ecclesial authority. In order to accomplish this revival, they wrote tracts, which were distributed throughout England and which soon gained adherents to their movement, especially among educated clergy and laymen. The efforts at renewal and orthodoxy met immediate resistance from the more liberal or "Broad Church" Anglicans as well as the Evangelicals. The latter were less concerned about these issues, but instead were primarily concerned with a demanding moral life and social reforms. The differences led to significant controversies in the election of professors at Oxford University and other disputes at Oxford. As leader of the movement, Newman played a prominent role in these events.

In addition to the tracts, the ideals of the Oxford Movement were defined and disseminated by Newman from the pulpit at St. Mary's University Church, where he was the rector. Although his sermons were about morals and piety, they were rooted in doctrine and Scripture, and on a vision of Christianity that was founded on objective truths. At St. Mary's, Newman also gave two series of lectures that further consolidated his beliefs and those of the movement. In one series, he explained the doctrine of justification through faith and works, correcting the Protestant version of justification by faith alone.

Newman was well acquainted with the seventeenth- and eighteenth-century Anglican theologians. From them, he learned Catholic principles. From the 1830s on, he began to seriously study the Church Fathers, men from the first nine centuries of Christianity known for their holiness of life and orthodox doctrine. From the Church Fathers,

Newman began to learn the importance of Tradition as a key to interpreting Scripture. He also came to recognize the need for apostolic succession — the unbroken transfer of sacramental and teaching authority in the Church — as a guarantee for the truth of doctrinal claims. Newman began to coordinate the translation of works of the Fathers into English. He grew in his knowledge and affection toward these early witnesses of Christianity.

In 1839, Newman decided to undertake a revision of his first book, *Arians of the Fourth Century*, on the ancient heresies and the councils of the early Church. In June of that year, while studying the fifth-century Monophysite heresy condemned by the Council of Chalcedon (451), his confidence in Anglicanism was first shaken. The Monophysites believed that Christ has only one nature: a divine nature. The writings and authority of Pope Leo the Great led to a definition of faith affirming that Christ has a divine nature and a human nature, which are perfectly united. Newman was struck by the moral authority of the pope that decided the outcome of the controversy at Chalcedon. Newman later wrote, "I saw my face in the mirror, and I was a Monophysite."[1] Newman told a friend that he was alarmed by discovering that Protestants and Anglicans were heretics like the Monophysites, and that he, too, was a heretic.[2] Until the fifth century, the criteria for choosing the authentic Church established by Christ was *antiquity*, but now that foundation was challenged. The test for a true Church was the authority of the See of Rome and its communion with the other churches.

Just when Newman was concluding his study of the Monophysite heresy, he began a history of the fifth-century Donatist schism in the African Church. This study further confirmed his finding that the judgments of the Roman See were definitive in deciding matters of the whole Church. Newman read an article by Nicholas Wiseman, "Tracts for the Times: Anglican Claim of Apostolical Succession," published in the *Dublin Review*. In the article, Wiseman argued that the Anglican Church was in schism from the true Church and thus could not claim apostolic succession.[3] Wiseman based his argument on those adduced by St. Augustine, St. Optatus, and St. Jerome against the Donatists, but he applied them to the Anglican Church and the Tractarians' "branch theory" — their claim that they were, like the Catholic and Orthodox Churches, another "branch" of the great Christian Tradition. In mid-September, a friend pointed out to Newman some key words in the article that had been taken from St. Augustine, words that had escaped Newman's observation: *Securus iudicat orbis terrarum*. The full sentence asserted: "Wherefore *the entire world judges with security* that they are not good who separate themselves from the entire world, in whatever part of the entire world."[4] Newman thus understood that just as much as antiquity, unity and apostolic succession decided which was the true Church.

Until this point, Newman held to the branch theory. Now, however, his distrust in Anglicanism was firm and permanent. Although he still tried, publicly, to defend the Anglican claim to be a branch of the true Church, it became clearer that the Roman Church's claim was true — that the Church of Rome was established by Christ. Roman Catholicism had antiquity, apostolic succession, and universality. The English Church lacked the latter two marks. It did not have the authority of Rome and unbroken succession of bishops with the See of Rome; and it was disunited from Christians of other parts of the world. In effect, the Church of England was in schism or separation from the main body of the Church. Newman, however, held out that the Church of England possessed signs of holiness, which he claimed that the Church of Rome did not have. Over time Newman came to see that the latter was untrue.

In 1840, he began spending more time at Littlemore, a hamlet within his parish, where he had built a small church, St. Mary Virgin and St. Nicholas. There he was able to live the season of Lent with greater recollection. In 1841, Newman moved to Littlemore; from there he could walk to Oxford for any business at Oriel College. Soon Newman bought property in Littlemore and adapted some barns as living quarters and a library. At Littlemore, a group of Tractarians, most of them undergraduates, gathered together with Newman to lead a life of prayer and study.

The year 1841 was a turning point for Newman. That year he published *Tract 90*, which attempted to show that the Thirty-Nine Articles — the authoritative constitution of the Anglican Church — could be interpreted without relinquishing Catholic principles. The publication of this tract caused a great opposition by liberal-minded members of Oxford University, and soon it led to criticism of the tract by one Anglican bishop after another. Newman agreed with the bishop of Oxford's request to cease publishing new tracts. Over the following years, attacks on Newman and the Tractarians continued, and Newman retired from public life at Oxford. He published some volumes of sermons and worked as editor of the *British Critic*.

In 1843, after having discussed the matter with his friend John Keble, Newman resigned as rector of St. Mary's University Church. Although Newman attempted to dissuade both his visitors at Littlemore and his correspondents from joining the Roman Catholic Church, Newman himself moved more toward the belief that this was indeed the true Church. He prayed and fasted, asking God for light and right judgment about this situation. At about this time, Newman began to take notes on the development in Christian doctrine over the centuries. In so doing, Newman realized that what he had thought were *corruptions* of primitive doctrines by Roman Catholics were in fact true *developments* of doctrine. Various events in ecclesiastical affairs — such as the creation of a joint Anglican-Lutheran See in Jerusalem (1841) and the censure of William G. Ward by the Oxford Convocation (1845), as well as a simultaneous attempt to censure *Tract 90* — convinced Newman of the untenable position of the Anglican Church as a branch of the true Church.

By September of 1845, when Newman was close to finishing his manuscript of *An Essay on the Development of Christian Doctrine*, he had decided to be received into full communion with the Church of Rome. He resigned his position as a fellow of Oriel College, and on October 9 became Roman Catholic. Father Dominic Barberi, a Passionist priest, heard his confession and profession of faith. (Father Barberi himself has been declared "Blessed" by the Catholic Church.) On that day, some of Newman's Littlemore companions also became Catholic. John Dalgairns and Ambrose St. John, friends and Littlemore companions, had preceded Newman by a few days.

Although expected, the news of Newman's reception into the Catholic Church was a blow to many of his friends and a source of mockery for liberal Anglicans who were glad to be rid of him. Wiseman, the Catholic bishop of the central region of England, encouraged Newman to study theology in Rome. Newman traveled with his fellow converts to Rome in 1846. On Trinity Sunday, May 30, 1846, Newman and Ambrose St. John were ordained Catholic priests by Cardinal Fransoni in the chapel of the college of Propaganda Fidei. After much consideration, Newman and his companions asked Blessed Pope Pius IX permission to start the Oratory of St. Philip Neri in England. They were inspired by the life of piety and charity of St. Philip, a sixteenth-century Italian priest. The pope granted them permission, and at the end of 1847 they returned to England to begin the Oratory, with Newman as superior. In 1849, the Oratory moved to Birmingham.

At the Birmingham Oratory, Newman administered the sacraments, gave talks, and guided the growth of the Oratory. For five years (1853-58), he traveled between Birmingham and Dublin, where he was entrusted by the Irish bishops with the difficult task of starting the Catholic University of Ireland. A shortage of students and lack of teachers compounded the difficulty of an Englishman starting a university among Irishmen. Another difficulty that Newman faced was opposition when he tried to give the laity a greater role in the day-to-day running of the university. Not long after resigning from the university that he had founded, Newman started a school for boys, the Oratory School in Birmingham. Later, at the request of William Ullathorne, bishop of Birmingham, he tried to open an Oratory in Oxford. He abandoned the project because the English bishops thought that studying at Oxford would endanger the faith of Catholic men.

Newman defended the Catholic Church in England on many occasions. Three stand out: his lectures *Present Position of English Catholics* (1850), when the English hierarchy was restored after centuries of suppression; his *Apologia Pro Vita Sua* (1864), which was as much a defense of Catholic doctrine as of his own life; and *The Letter to the Duke of Norfolk* (1875). As evidenced in these important works, Newman's passion and intelligence, his deep knowledge of history, and his prose style were unparalleled. For these reasons, at the request of the Duke of Norfolk and other English nobles, Pope Leo XIII elevated Newman to the dignity of cardinal. He received the cardinal's hat in 1879.

Newman continued to reside at the Birmingham Oratory, where he received visits, answered questions posed to him, and wrote. His health declined with the passing of years, and he died on August 11, 1890.

All of England mourned the death of this great priest and intellectual.

Newman's Contributions

John Henry Newman's rich life and teaching elude easy summary. He was a historian, a theologian, a pastor, a loyal friend, and a philosopher. Although he did not write theological treatises, he made contributions to fundamental theology, moral theology, ecclesiology (the study of the Church), and biblical theology. In this book, we would like to point out other salient points in his teaching for which he is justly remembered:

1. **The pursuit of objective religious truth.** In nineteenth-century England, the fashionable philosophy fostered a skeptical attitude that was scornful of religion. The Industrial Revolution gave some people a false sense of confidence in technological progress and led them to relegate religion to subjective opinion. Even religious leaders began to express doubts about the authority of the Bible and the objective nature of religious truth. Newman countered that God gave the world an oracle of truth, which is the Church. He argued that the successor of Peter had the authority to provide definitive ruling on matters of faith and morals. In his essays, he

unmasked false assumptions, generalizations, and conclusions that attempted to trivialize and relativize religious truths. The ideas he opposed have not disappeared, but rather found new disguises. Newman's arguments, though, are ever new.

2. **Teaching on the virtues.** To his students and his parishioners, Newman emphasized the importance of the supernatural and moral virtues. His teaching was rooted in the biblical texts and presented the example of Jesus Christ and the apostles, as well as figures from the Old Testament. He taught about all the virtues, although he placed special attention on the theological virtues: faith, hope, and charity. Newman's preaching on this subject was based on his life experience and personal effort to live the virtues. It was the result of personal self-examination and a daily effort to earnestly live a Christian life. As a keen observer, Newman offered his listeners many insights into human psychology and the fight against temptations. He placed before his parishioners or readers the final goal — eternal life — as the reference point for the practice of the virtues. At the same time, Newman's exposition of the virtues was concrete and practical; it was attractive and real.

3. **Defense of the Catholic Church.** Newman believed that the Church's origin and ends are supernatural. He taught that the Church's teaching is authoritative. As a convert, Newman felt the need to defend the Church from unjust accusations and anti-Catholic bigotry. He did this by presenting historical evidence in favor of the Church and by unmasking false arguments. He defended the Church both in lectures and in writing. Today, too, there is a pressing need to defend the Church from false and harmful attacks. Newman gives us a good example of a courageous defender of the faith, as well as useful tools for this noble purpose. If Newman lived in today's world, he would probably have an impressive website and active blog!

4. **A devout spiritual and moral life.** John Henry Newman is well known for his intellectual genius. He published many scholarly books in his lifetime and advanced theological points concerning faith and reason, the moral conscience, and the theology of the Church. Yet Newman's life cannot be correctly understood apart from his religious devotion and exemplary moral life. Newman preached what he lived: a clear devotion to the Blessed Trinity, a strong

eucharistic piety, a love for the sacraments, an awareness of the Communion of Saints, as well as the practice of Christian charity. Those who knew him attested to his high standard of moral behavior and Christian life, which gave force to his written and spoken words.

5. **Generosity and loyalty in his friendships.** All men and women value friendship, but Christians, in particular, should have a deeper understanding of respect and charity in friendship. These attributes characterize Newman's friendships. Though timid by nature, Newman was affectionate and sincere, and he developed many friendships throughout his long life. Naturally, his friendships arose out of common interests: related studies as well as shared experiences and, especially, common religious beliefs. Soon the young Oxford don became a leader among his friends, and he was frequently sought out for advice. He was generous in helping friends by replying to their questions and concerns.

In the time when Newman was at Oxford, the university admitted only men; and many college teachers considered higher education so demanding that they chose to observe celibacy. Newman developed strong bonds of friendship with his peers, such as John Bowden and Richard Hurrell Froude, and later with others, like John Dalgairns and Ambrose St. John. Even in Newman's own lifetime, his enemies sometimes falsely portrayed his friendships as homosexual relationships. The matter was investigated, and there is no evidence to indicate that Newman had homosexual inclinations, much less homosexual relations. His conscientious practice of Christian morality and his life of prayer would have precluded any unchaste behavior on his part.

Newman's desire to remain celibate was in no way due to insecurity about his sexuality. His choice to remain single was based on the firm desire from his early adulthood to serve God with the greater freedom that celibate life affords. Newman did not disdain marriage. Some of his closest friends — such as John Keble and Edward Pusey — were married. He briefly lamented the marriage of his friend William Henry Wilberforce, but only because he felt this was a loss for the Anglican Church in need of celibate clergy. During his life, Newman had good friendships with both single and married women, whom he came to know through his male friends.

Newman was a loyal friend. He stood by his friends when they needed assistance of any type. He was always ready to serve them. He prayed for them and offered them spiritual advice when opportune. He visited them and comforted them when they were ill or suffered the loss of loved ones. More than thirty volumes of letters and diary entries introduce readers into the vast world of Newman's friendships. One can only imagine how many e-mails he would have written if he could have lived in the twenty-first century. Many of his letters reveal the closeness and spontaneity, as well as the warm affection, of his numerous friendships.

Newman chose as a motto a phrase from St. Francis de Sales: *Cor ad cor loquitur* ("Heart speaks to heart"). It is no surprise that the motto he chose was about friendship. Newman believed that true friends communicate, heart to heart, what is important in life. He was shy in any group of more than a few people, but in one-on-one conversations and in letters Newman opened his heart and his mind. A remarkable intellectual and author, he was, above all, a very good Christian and a true friend.

Notes

1. John Henry Newman, *Apologia Pro Vita Sua,* 114.

2. Ibid., 114-115.

3. Nicholas Wiseman, "The Anglican Claim of Apostolic Succession" in the *Dublin Review,* 1839, quoted from *Publications of the Catholic Truth Society,* Vol. XXIV, 1895, 7-56.

4. St. Augustine, *Cont. Epist. Parmen*, lib. iii, cap. 3; quoted in ibid., 23. Emphasis added.

References

CITATIONS OF NEWMAN'S WORKS

Newman, John Henry. *Letters and Diaries.* Edited by Charles Stephen Dessain, Ian Ker, Thomas Gornall, Edward E. Kelly, Gerard Tracey, and Francis J. McGrath (Oxford: Clarendon Press, 1978-2006).

———. Newman's Works, "Uniform Edition" (London: Longmans, Green, and Co., 1900-1910).

SOURCES CONSULTED

Newman, John Henry. Newman Reader, *www.newmanreader.org.*

———. *The Rule of Our Warfare: John Henry Newman and the True Christian Life.* John Hulsman, ed. (New York: Scepter Publishers, 2003).

BIOGRAPHIES

Ker, Ian. *John Henry Newman: A Biography* (Oxford: Oxford University Press, 1988).

Morales, José. *Newman 1801-1890* (Madrid: Ediciones Rialp, 1990).

Trevor, Meriol. *Newman*. Vol. 1, *The Pillar of the Cloud*; Vol. 2, *Light in Winter* (Garden City, NY: Doubleday, 1962-63).

Ward, Maisie. *Young Mr. Newman* (New York: Sheed & Ward, 1948).

Abbreviations

Addresses	Addresses to Cardinal Newman with His Replies
DA	Discussions and Arguments
Dev	Essay on the Development of Christian Doctrine
Diff	Difficulties Faced by Anglicans
GA	Grammar of Assent
Idea	Idea of a University
LD	Letters and Diaries of John Henry Newman
MD	Meditations and Devotions
Mix	Discourses to Mixed Congregations
OS	Sermons Preached on Various Occasions
PPS	Parochial and Plain Sermons
Prepos	Present Positions of English Catholics
Rambler	Contributions of John Henry Newman
Sayings	Sayings of Cardinal Newman
SD	Sermons on Subjects of the Day
VV	Verses on Various Occasions

Everyone seeks happiness, yet many people do not find it. They look for it in the wrong places.

This is our real and true bliss, not to know, or to affect, or to pursue; but to love, to hope, to joy, to admire, to revere, to adore. Our real and true bliss lies in the possession of those objects on which our hearts may rest and be satisfied.

Now, if this be so, here is at once a reason for saying that the thought of God, and nothing short of it, is the happiness of man; for though there is much besides to serve as subject of knowledge, or motive for action, or means of excitement, yet the affections require a something more vast and more enduring than anything created. What is novel and sudden excites, but does not influence; what is pleasurable or useful raises no awe; self moves no reverence, and mere knowledge kindles no love. He alone is sufficient for the heart who made it.

PPS, 5:116

THINK ABOUT IT

- There is no lasting satisfaction except for God. All joys are fleeting without God.
- Do I think of God often and consider that my ultimate happiness must be rooted in God?

■ If I am often disappointed, it is probably because I seek from others what only God can give.

And now, my sons, listen to me:
     happy are those who keep my ways....
Happy is the man who listens to me,
     watching daily at my gates,
     waiting beside my doors.

PROVERBS 8:32, 34

Set me as a seal upon your heart,
     as a seal upon your arm.

SONG OF SOLOMON 8:6

The thought of God, and nothing short of it, is our happiness.

2. The World Is Too Small to Satisfy Us

God created us with a longing that is infinite, a longing only he can fill. The things of this world are finite and imperfect.

I do not say, of course, that nothing short of the Almighty Creator can awaken and answer to our love, reverence, and trust; man can do this for man … our hearts require something more permanent and uniform than man can be. We gain much for a time from fellowship with each other. It is a relief to us, as fresh air to the fainting, or meat and drink to the hungry, or a flood of tears to the heavy in mind. It is a soothing comfort to have those whom we may make our confidants; a comfort to have those to whom we may confess our faults; a comfort to have those to whom we may look for sympathy. Love of home and family in these and other ways is sufficient to make this life tolerable to the multitude of men, which otherwise it would not be; but still, after all, our affections exceed such exercise of them, and demand what is more stable.

PPS, 5:313-316

THINK ABOUT IT

- As great as human love can be, we were made for something even greater.

- Do I ever make an idol of friendship, family, or fellowship?
- When I suffer, do I seek consolation from God as well as friends and family?

For God alone my soul waits in silence;
    from him comes my salvation.
He only is my rock and my salvation,
    my fortress; I shall not be greatly moved.

PSALM 62:1-2

Earthly love is sufficient to make life tolerable, which otherwise it would not be; but our affections demand much more.

Only God knows our thoughts and can enter us.

But there is another reason why God alone is the happiness of our souls, to which I wish rather to direct attention: the contemplation of Him, and nothing but it, is able fully to open and relieve the mind, to unlock, occupy, and fix our affections. We may indeed love things created with great intenseness, but such affection, when disjoined from the love of the Creator, is like a stream running in a narrow channel, impetuous, vehement, turbid. The heart runs out, as it were, only at one door; it is not an expanding of the whole man. Created natures cannot open us, or elicit the ten thousand mental senses which belong to us, and through which we really live. None but the presence of our Maker can enter us; for to none besides can the whole heart in all its thoughts and feelings be unlocked and subjected.

PPS, 5:317-318

THINK ABOUT IT

- Is my love of created things and people subordinate to my love of God?
- Do my earthly affections serve to build me up spiritually?
- I must come to know God as the only key to my thoughts and feelings.

O LORD, thou hast searched me and
    known me!
Thou knowest when I sit down and when
    I rise up;
    thou discernest my thoughts from afar.
Thou searchest out my path and my
    lying down,
    and art acquainted with all my ways.

PSALM 139:1-3

REMEMBER

None but our Maker can enter us. None but our Maker can unlock the whole heart in all its thoughts and feelings.

4. God Is Always There

From his youth, Newman had a strong awareness of God's greatness and presence in the world.

It is this feeling of simple and absolute confidence and communion, which soothes and satisfies those to whom it is [given]. We know that even our nearest friends enter into us but partially, and hold [conversation] with us only at times; whereas the consciousness of a perfect and enduring Presence, and it alone, keeps the heart open. Withdraw the Object on which it rests, and it will relapse again into its state of confinement and constraint; and in proportion as it is limited, either to certain seasons or to certain affections, the heart is straitened and distressed. If it be not over bold to say it, He who is infinite can alone be its measure; He alone can answer to the mysterious assemblage of feelings and thoughts which it has within it.

PPS, 5:318-319

THINK ABOUT IT

- Only an infinite object — only God — can keep my heart from becoming cramped and confined.
- I must remember often that God is with me and look to him as the measure of my heart.
- My soul aspires to the Infinite, to God, who is Truth, Beauty, and Goodness.

[Christ] is the image of the invisible God, the first-born of all creation; for in him all things were created, in heaven and on earth, visible and invisible, whether thrones or dominions or principalities or authorities — all things were created through him and for him. He is before all things, and in him all things hold together.

COLOSSIANS 1:15-17

REMEMBER

Only the One who is infinite can be the measure of the heart.

Many people look for warm and fuzzy feelings in religion. They choose beliefs that are comfortable. Newman warned against such indulgence in soft religion.

We are alarmed at any call to national or personal humiliation and amendment; we like to be told of the excellence of our institutions, we do not like to hear of their defects; we like to abandon ourselves to the satisfactions of religion, we do not like to hear of its severities. We do not like to hear of our past sins, and the necessity of undoing them; and thus, however gay our blossoms may be in this our spring, we have a fault within which will show itself ere our fruits are gathered in the autumn....

We are cherishing a shallow religion, a hollow religion, which will not profit us in the day of trouble.... I said then, as now, that the age, whatever be its peculiar excellences, has this serious defect, it loves an exclusively cheerful religion. It is determined to make religion bright and sunny and joyous, whatever be the form of it which it adopts. And it will handle the Catholic doctrine in this spirit; it will skim over it; it will draw it out in mere buckets-full; it will substitute its human cistern for the well of truth; it will be afraid of the deep well, the abyss of God's judgments and God's mercies.

SD, 116-117

- Does my Christian life include the practice of penance — that is, sacrifices to make up for my sins and the sins of others?
- I must not permit myself to forget the judgment of God.
- The truth is good for me, even when it makes me feel uncomfortable.

JUST IMAGINE

"Enter by the narrow gate; for the gate is wide and the way is easy, that leads to destruction, and those who enter by it are many. For the gate is narrow and the way is hard, that leads to life, and those who find it are few."

MATTHEW 7:13-14

REMEMBER

Shallow religion will not profit us in the day of trouble.

The mark of true Christians is to watch — to be attentive to Christ as to a dearest friend.

Do you know what it is so to live upon a person who is present with you, that your eyes follow his, that you read his soul, that you see all its changes in his countenance, that you anticipate his wishes, that you smile in his smile, and are sad in his sadness, and are downcast when he is vexed, and rejoice in his successes? To watch for Christ is a feeling such as all these; as far as feelings of this world are fit to shadow out those of another.

He watches for Christ who has a sensitive, eager, apprehensive mind; who is awake, alive, quick-sighted, zealous in seeking and honoring Him; who looks out for Him in all that happens, and who would not be surprised, who would not be over-agitated or overwhelmed, if he found that He was coming at once.

PPS, 4:323-324

THINK ABOUT IT

- I should at least desire to want what Christ wants.
- Do I seek Christ's friendship?
- Do I live in a manner that I would not be surprised by his sudden appearance?

"No longer do I call you servants, for the servant does not know what his master is doing; but I have called you friends, for all that I have heard from my Father I have made known to you."

JOHN 15:15

I wish not to be surprised, "over-agitated," or overwhelmed, if I found that Christ was coming at once.

7. Progress Through Virtues

Christian perfection calls for the daily effort to practice the virtues. The majority of Newman's sermons touched on the theological and moral virtues.

There are many persons who proceed a little way in religion, and then stop short. God keep us from choking the good seed, which else would come to perfection! Let us exercise ourselves in those good works, which both reverse the evil that is past, and lay up a good foundation for us in the world to come.

SD, 51

THINK ABOUT IT

- Am I making an effort to advance in my Christian life?
- Do I consider that the good seed of faith needs to be watered in order to grow?
- God expects that we develop good habits such as order, responsibility, patience, cheerfulness, justice, generosity, etc.

JUST IMAGINE

Put on then, as God's chosen ones, holy and beloved, compassion, kindness, lowliness, meekness, and patience.

COLOSSIANS 3:12

There are many people who proceed a little way in religion, and then stop short.

8. Be Sincere and Humble Before God

Self-knowledge leads to humility, which is a necessary condition for spiritual growth. When we realize our great need, we seek God's grace.

Let us pray God to teach us: we need His teaching; we are very blind. The Apostles on one occasion said to Christ, when His words tried them, "Increase our faith." Let us come to Him honestly: we cannot help ourselves; we do not know ourselves; we need His grace.

SD, 77

THINK ABOUT IT

- Do I recognize my utter dependence upon God?
- God responds to all humble prayers.
- Before God, I am a beggar.

JUST IMAGINE

But she came and knelt before him, saying, "Lord, help me."

MATTHEW 15:25

REMEMBER

We cannot help ourselves; we do not know ourselves; we need God's grace.

9. The Snares of Pride

Pride is a constant danger. True humility is difficult to achieve. As a college student and afterward a tutor at Oriel College, Newman was often tempted by intellectual pride. He shows us some of the traps that lurk.

Many a man instead of *learning* humility in practice, confesses himself a poor sinner, and next *prides* himself upon the confession; he ascribes the glory of his redemption to God, and then becomes in a manner *proud* that he is redeemed. He is proud of his so-called humility.... We think ourselves wise; we flatter each other; we make excuses for ourselves when we are conscious we sin, and thus we gradually lose the consciousness that we are sinning. We think our own times superior to all others.

PPS, 1:28, 39

THINK ABOUT IT

- Do I recognize in myself daily manifestations of pride and vanity?
- Do I think of myself as better than others and seek people's flattery?
- To accept my limitations and to recognize my errors are ways to grow in humility.

"Whoever humbles himself like this child, he is the greatest in the kingdom of heaven."

MATTHEW 18:4

REMEMBER

We think ourselves wise; we flatter each other; we make excuses for ourselves when we are conscious we sin.

*St. Paul said, "Faith, hope, love abide, these three;
but the greatest of these is love" (1 Corinthians 13:13).
Newman tells us what's so different about love.*

Faith and hope are graces of an imperfect state,
and they cease with that state; but love is greater,
because it is perfection. Faith and hope are graces,
as far as we belong to this world — which is for a
time; but love is a grace, because we are creatures of
God whether here or elsewhere, and partakers in a
redemption which is to last for ever. Faith will not be
when there is sight, nor hope when there is enjoyment;
but love will (as we believe) increase more and more
to all eternity. Faith and hope are means by which
we express our love: we believe God's word, because
we love it; we hope after heaven, because we love it.
We should not have any hope or concern about it,
unless we loved it; we should not trust or confide
in the God of heaven, unless we loved Him. Faith,
then, and hope are but instruments or expressions of
love; but as to love itself, we do not love because we
believe, for the devils believe, yet do not love; nor do
we love because we hope, for hypocrites hope, who
do not love. But we love for no cause beyond itself:
we love, because it is our nature to love; and it is our
nature, because God the Holy Ghost has made it our

nature. Love is the immediate fruit and the evidence of regeneration.

PPS, 4:309-310

THINK ABOUT IT

- Do I understand what the saints mean by "love"?
- Do I make the virtue of love primary in my life?
- In what aspects of my life do I frequently fail to live charity?

JUST IMAGINE

Beloved, let us love one another; for love is of God, and he who loves is born of God and knows God. He who does not love does not know God; for God is love. In this the love of God was made manifest among us, that God sent his only Son into the world, so that we might live through him.

1 JOHN 4:7-9

REMEMBER

But we love for no cause beyond itself: we love, because it is our nature to love; and it is our nature, because God the Holy Ghost has made it our nature.

11. Understand and Accept Others

Charity bids us to understand others' character and accept their differences and shortcomings. Newman made friends of people with a wide range of personalities and tastes.

There is a great deal to do in the way of disciplining our hearts, which we only gain by being brought together. Everyone likes his own way; and, of course, it becomes an impossibility for everyone to have his own way when there are a great many to be consulted. And, therefore, the very collision of mind with mind is a great advantage. And though it brings a soul into a certain degree of temptation, yet it is a temptation which turns to good from its being wrestled with and overcome. And another advantage is that we all have our own tastes, our likes and dislikes; and no number of minds can come together without having their likings and dislikings overcome. We have to look at things in a higher light.

Sayings, 70

THINK ABOUT IT

- Do I try to better understand family members and co-workers?
- Do I accept all people with their likes and dislikes?

- I should try to accommodate to others in matters that are open to opinion.

JUST IMAGINE

Love is patient and kind; love is not jealous or boastful; it is not arrogant or rude. Love does not insist on its own way; it is not irritable or resentful; it does not rejoice at wrong, but rejoices in the right. Love bears all things, believes all things, hopes all things, endures all things.

1 Corinthians 13:4-7

REMEMBER

We have to look at things in a higher light.

12. Conscience: God's Voice

Newman had a high regard for individual conscience. He defended its nature against the misunderstandings of many people, including materialists who would reduce conscience to mere enlightened self-interest. It is, rather, God's voice.

Conscience is not a long-sighted selfishness, nor a desire to be consistent with oneself; but it is a messenger from Him, who, both in nature and in grace, speaks to us behind a veil, and teaches and rules us by His representatives. Conscience is the aboriginal Vicar of Christ, a prophet in its informations, a monarch in its peremptoriness, a priest in its blessings and anathemas, and, even though the eternal priesthood throughout the Church could cease to be, in it the sacerdotal principle would remain and would have a sway.

Diff, II, 248-249

THINK ABOUT IT

■ Do I examine my own conscience to see that it conforms to the Church's teaching?

■ Do I respect the freedom of others to follow the dictates of their conscience?

■ I should ask the Holy Spirit for light to make correct judgments of conscience and thus use my freedom well.

For freedom Christ has set us free; stand fast therefore, and do not submit again to a yoke of slavery.... For you were called to freedom, brethren; only do not use your freedom as an opportunity for the flesh, but through love be servants of one another.

GALATIANS 5:1, 13

REMEMBER

Conscience is a messenger from Christ.

13. The World as Witness

Christianity is not a theory. It is a historical fact, and history is its witness.

Christianity has been long enough in the world to justify us in dealing with it as a fact in the world's history. Its genius and character, its doctrines, precepts, and objects cannot be treated as matters of private opinion or deduction, ... unless the testimony of so many centuries is to go for nothing. Christianity is no theory of the study or the cloister. It has long since passed beyond the letter of documents and the reasonings of individual minds, and has become public property. Its "sound has gone out into all lands," and its "words unto the ends of the world." It has from the first had an objective existence, and has thrown itself upon the great concourse of men. Its home is in the world; and to know what it is, we must seek it in the world, and hear the world's witness of it.

Dev, 3-4

THINK ABOUT IT

- With the Incarnation, Christ entered history and embraced our humanity.
- Can I respond intelligently to those who misconstrue events in Christian history?

■ We must learn about the decisive contributions of Christianity to the world of culture, education, family life, science, government, and public life.

In those days a decree went out from Caesar Augustus that all the world should be enrolled. This was the first enrollment, when Quirinius was governor of Syria. And all went to be enrolled, each to his own city. And Joseph also went up from Galilee, from the city of Nazareth, to Judea, to the city of David, which is called Bethlehem, because he was of the house and lineage of David, to be enrolled with Mary, his betrothed, who was with child. And while they were there, the time came for her to be delivered. And she gave birth to her first-born son and wrapped him in swaddling cloths, and laid him in a manger, because there was no place for them in the inn.

LUKE 2:1-7

REMEMBER

Christianity's home is in the world; and to know what it is, we must seek it in the world, and hear the world's witness of it.

14. Deep in History

Even before Newman became a Catholic, he recognized that history did not support a Protestant conception of early Christian history.

[Protestant] popular religion scarcely recognizes the fact of the twelve long ages which lie between the Councils of Nicæa and Trent, except as affording one or two passages to illustrate its wild interpretations of certain prophesies of St. Paul and St. John. It is melancholy to say it, but the chief, perhaps the only English writer who has any claim to be considered an ecclesiastical historian, is the unbeliever Gibbon. To be deep in history is to cease to be a Protestant.

Dev, 7-8

THINK ABOUT IT

- Do I know much about the early roots of the papacy, the sacraments, and other distinctively Catholic doctrines and practices?
- To be an effective Christian witness, I need to know about the history of Christianity.
- I wish to be "deep in history," because God entered human history, and the truth entrusted to men is embedded in that human history.

Inasmuch as many have undertaken to compile a narrative of the things which have been accomplished among us, just as they were delivered to us by those who from the beginning were eyewitnesses and ministers of the word, it seemed good to me also, having followed all things closely for some time past, to write an orderly account for you, most excellent Theophilus, that you may know the truth concerning the things of which you have been informed.

LUKE 1:1-4

To be deep in history is to be ever more firmly a Catholic.

15. Beyond Study: Prayer and Fasting

Study is good, but it gets us only so far. Newman advised a spiritual inquirer to put aside his intellectual investigations for a time and devote himself to spiritual means.

If I might venture to suggest, I would say that, were I in your present most painful state of mind, I think I should give over the *direct inquiry* for several years and give myself to fasting and prayer and practical duties. At the end of this time I trust that God would enlighten my judgment — at all events I should be in a better state of mind to judge how my duty lay.

LD, 7:404

THINK ABOUT IT

- Do I study the truths of the Catholic faith?
- Do I give myself the time to think and pray through problems and difficulties? And do I accept that I cannot expect to solve every difficulty?
- Many times it is through renunciation, prayer, and fasting that I can gain clarity and learn humility.

Saul arose from the ground; and when his eyes were opened, he could see nothing; so they led him by the hand and brought him into Damascus. And for three days he was without sight, and neither ate nor drank.... And laying his hands on him [Ananias] said, "Brother Saul, the Lord Jesus who appeared to you on the road by which you came, has sent me that you may regain your sight and be filled with the Holy Spirit."

ACTS 9:8-9, 17

There is a time to put direct inquiry on hold and give myself to prayer and practical duties.

16. Trust in Religious Truths

Already in the nineteenth century, Newman refuted the claim that modern sciences can determine religious truths. Newman tried to delineate the limits of such sciences.

Science gives us the grounds or premises from which religious truths are to be inferred; but it does not set about inferring them, much less does it reach the inference — that is not its province. It brings before us phenomena, and it leaves us, if we will, to call them works of design, wisdom, or benevolence; and further still, if we will, to proceed to confess an Intelligent Creator. We have to take its facts, and to give them a meaning, and to draw our own conclusions from them.

GA, 92

THINK ABOUT IT

- Modern science is not greater than religion nor is good science opposed to religion.
- Do I trust science more than religious truths?
- We are saved by love, not by science or technology.

JUST IMAGINE

For what can be known about God is plain to them, because God has shown it to them. Ever since the creation of the world his invisible nature, namely, his eternal power and deity, has been clearly perceived in the things that have been made. So they are without excuse.

ROMANS 1:19-20

REMEMBER

We have to take science's facts, and to give them a meaning, and to draw our own conclusions from them.

17. Faith's Power of Persuasion

Newman articulated the idea that man knows spiritual realities by multiple impressions and associations of the mind and heart, and the witness of people and events, which together he called the "illative sense."

First comes knowledge, then a view, then reasoning, and then belief. This is why science has so little of a religious tendency; deductions have no power of persuasion. The heart is commonly reached, not through the reason, but through the imagination, by means of direct impressions, by the testimony of facts and events, by history, by description. Persons influence us, voices melt us, looks subdue us, deeds inflame us. Many a man will live and die upon a dogma: no man will be a martyr for a conclusion.

GA, 92-93

THINK ABOUT IT

- Faith is much more than a deduction.
- God reaches man's heart in many ways.
- Religious dogma calls for real commitment.

JUST IMAGINE

And when Jesus came to the place, he looked up and said to him, "Zacchaeus, make haste and come down; for I must stay at your house today."

So he made haste and came down, and received him joyfully.

LUKE 19:5-6

REMEMBER

The heart is commonly reached, not through the reason, but through the imagination, by means of direct impressions, by the testimony of facts and events, by history, by description. People influence us, voices melt us, looks subdue us.

18. The Greatest Science

Theology is the highest science because it is the science of God. Even educated Catholics, however, neglect its study. Newman thought it should be taught at every university.

Religious doctrine is knowledge, in as full a sense as Newton's doctrine is knowledge. University Teaching without Theology is simply unphilosophical. Theology has at least as good a right to claim a place there as Astronomy.

Idea, 42

THINK ABOUT IT

- Am I aware that theology is truly a science, the ordered study of a thing by its causes?
- Do I realize that the study of created things in every university discipline bears a relation to theology?
- University studies without natural theology are incomplete and misguided.

JUST IMAGINE

I do not cease to give thanks for you, remembering you in my prayers, that the God of our Lord Jesus Christ, the Father of glory, may give you a spirit of wisdom and of revelation in the knowledge of him, having the eyes of your hearts enlightened.

EPHESIANS 1:16-18

REMEMBER

An education without theology is simply unphilosophical.

19. Holiness in Everyday life

Newman advised lay Catholics to be a leaven in society. Holiness, however, begins with a personal, interior struggle to fight sin and grow in virtue. When asked about a recent convert who wished to write books, Newman counseled that she should tend first to her soul.

Let her turn her activity and energy upon herself; let her consider how much must be done by every one of us to enter life; how much is open to everyone to do both to the glory of God and towards personal improvement; how high and wonderful a thing Christian sanctity is; and what capabilities the regenerate soul has for improvement.

LD, 7:335

THINK ABOUT IT

- Out of love for God, do I strive to improve daily?
- Have I given in to laziness and false contentment in any area of my spiritual life: prayer, study, or the practice of Christian virtues?
- I must resolve to honor God, recognizing the greatness of Christian life to which he calls me.

JUST IMAGINE

But grow in the grace and knowledge of our Lord and Savior Jesus Christ. To him be the glory both now and to the day of eternity. Amen.

2 PETER 3:18

REMEMBER

Consider how much can be done both for the glory of God and my own improvement.

Newman advised friends to study the basic, classic books of spirituality and lives of the saints, and then to reshape their worldview accordingly. Here is his counsel for a friend who wished to set a program for a newly converted woman.

[She should] give herself to the contemplation of obedience and holiness, and the reading of the lives of the saints; and set herself deliberately to the business of self-government, of changing herself where she most requires it, of gaining perfect resignation to God's will, of unlearning worldly opinions, motives and principles, and of living as if in the sight of things invisible — and that without impatience at apparent failure or apparent slow advance.

LD, 7:335-336

THINK ABOUT IT

- Do I have a firm grasp of the basics of Catholic life, prayer, and doctrine?
- Do I seek good guidance when I choose material for spiritual reading?
- Before going after novelties and fads, it's best to give the saints a hearing.

I fed you with milk, not solid food; for you were not ready for it; and even yet you are not ready.

1 Corinthians 3:2

Like newborn babes, long for the pure spiritual milk, that by it you may grow up to salvation.

1 Peter 2:2

Read the lives of the saints, and live as if in the sight of things invisible.

21. Make Small Sacrifices

Newman fasted regularly, and sometimes rigorously. Still, he advised others not to attempt anything heroic, but instead to make small, unnoticed acts of self-denial at meals.

I would not abstain from food in a way to attract attention — but there are ways of denying oneself, where no one would suspect it.

LD, 7:341-342

THINK ABOUT IT

- I should try not to be noticed and praised for my piety.
- My prayers are for God's glory, not mine.
- Are there small sacrifices I can make quietly, every day?

JUST IMAGINE

[Jesus said:] "And when you fast, do not look dismal, like the hypocrites, for they disfigure their faces that their fasting may be seen by men. Truly, I say to you, they have their reward. But when you fast, anoint your head and wash your face, that your fasting may not be seen by men but by your Father who is in secret; and your Father who sees in secret will reward you."

MATTHEW 6:16-18

Deny yourself where no one would suspect it.

22. Fight, Not Flight

Newman realized that sin is not primarily caused by "the world," but rather by indulging in a disordered attraction to the good things of the world. He insisted that we must fight temptations with eyes set on heaven. He counseled one influential woman not to flee from the world.

I do not think advisable you should break off your usual visits to the Court — particularly as your stay is limited. Nothing in the course of engagements in which you find yourself is actually objectionable, and therefore you should continue in them.

LD, 7:361

THINK ABOUT IT

- Do I consider that the world created by God is good?
- Do I recognize the good I can do in places where I am perhaps the only believer?
- I must look for opportunities to be a Christian witness in my work.

JUST IMAGINE

Greet every saint in Christ Jesus. The brethren who are with me greet you. All the saints greet you, especially those of Caesar's household.

PHILIPPIANS 4:21-22

Where nothing is objectionable, continue your presence.

23. Self-Examination

Newman advocated the practice of self-examination and self-control. He told one of his friends that she need not live in a convent to overcome temptations.

Though temptations present themselves to you in society, you would soon find temptations in solitude, were you to indulge your love of it. We cannot escape from *ourselves,* wherever we are — and *we* are the sinners, not the places in which we find ourselves.

LD, 7:361

THINK ABOUT IT

- I must uncover my strongest temptations and, with God's help, fight against them.
- I should examine my conscience every day and make an act of contrition.
- What is the dominant fault that leads me to many of my other failings?

JUST IMAGINE

Whoever, therefore, eats the bread or drinks the cup of the Lord in an unworthy manner will be guilty of profaning the body and blood of the Lord. Let a man examine himself, and so eat of the bread and drink of the cup.

1 Corinthians 11:27-28

REMEMBER

We cannot escape from ourselves, wherever we are —
and we are the sinners, not the places in which we
find ourselves.

24. Check Your Emotions

Newman urged a young lay person to use her reason to take prayerful control of her passions and emotions, and not to be so affected by the opinions of others.

All your powers of mind and capacities of usefulness will go for nothing, till you use them. They will war against each other, like a country in insurrection. You are in one frame of mind one day, another the next. You depend on what people say of you.

LD, 9:319

THINK ABOUT IT

- Do I worry too much about what people think of me?
- Am I impulsive in the way I express my feelings?
- I should discipline myself to avoid looking for others' approval and to govern the expression of my emotions.

JUST IMAGINE

Many ... of the authorities believed in him, but for fear of the Pharisees they did not confess it, lest they should be put out of the synagogue: for they loved the praise of men more than the praise of God.

JOHN 12:42-43

All my powers will war against one another, if I depend on what people say of me.

We should not invoke a right to private judgment in order to contradict objective truth. If the Church's faith is from God, we have no right to judge it.

Immediate, implicit submission of the mind was, in the lifetime of the Apostles, the only, the necessary token of faith; then there was no room whatever for what is now called private judgment. No one could say: "I will choose my religion for myself, I will believe this, I will not believe that; I will pledge myself to nothing; I will believe just as long as I please, and no longer...." No; either the Apostles were from God, or they were not; if they were, everything that they preached was to be believed by their hearers; if they were not, there was nothing for their hearers to believe.... [T]hey [the Apostles] were nothing in themselves, they were all things, they were an infallible authority, as coming from God. The world had either to become Christian, or to let it alone; there was no room for private tastes and fancies, no room for private judgment.

Mix, 197

THINK ABOUT IT

■ A "cafeteria" approach to the faith is neither Catholic nor Christian.

- I must not make myself the judge of God's revelation or of his apostles.
- Do I hesitate to submit my mind to the rightful authority established by Christ?

JUST IMAGINE

[Jesus said to the apostles:] "He who receives you receives me, and he who receives me receives him who sent me."

MATTHEW 10:40

REMEMBER

In faith, there is no room whatever for what is now called private judgment.

26. Conversion: A Question of Truth

Some people complained that conversion was causing disunity in families. Newman responded that it is a wake-up call.

The disunion of families indeed remains, and it is enough to turn one's head; but in proportion as one feels confident that a change is right, in the same proportion one wishes others to change too; and though it is anything but my wish that they should change because I do, of course it cannot pain me that they should take my change as a sort of warning, or call to consider where the Truth lies.

LD, 10:591

THINK ABOUT IT

- On earth it is inevitable that families will be divided with respect to religious truths.
- In matters of faith and morals, am I ready to put God before my family?
- Do I help new converts who are estranged from their families?

JUST IMAGINE

[Jesus said:] "They will be divided, father against son and son against father, mother against daughter and daughter against her mother, mother-in-law against her daughter-in-law and daughter-in-law against her mother-in-law."

Luke 12:53

REMEMBER

Take change as a sort of warning, or a call to consider where the Truth lies.

27. The Joy of Seeing God

Happiness on earth is incomplete. Everything is subject to change and decay. Only the encounter with God in heaven can bring full and lasting joy. Newman comforted a friend whose wife died following a long illness.

After the fever of life; after wearinesses and sicknesses; fightings and despondings; languor and fretfulness; struggling and failing, struggling and succeeding; after all the changes and chances of this troubled unhealthy state, at length comes death, at length the White Throne of God, at length the Beatific Vision. After restlessness comes rest, peace, joy — our eternal portion, if we be worthy.

PPS, 6:369-370

THINK ABOUT IT

- The Christian vision of faith transforms suffering from illness and the grief over the loss of loved ones.
- How deeply do I believe what has been revealed about eternal life?
- We should pray for words of consolation when friends are mourning.

He will wipe away every tear from their eyes, and death shall be no more, neither shall there be mourning nor crying nor pain any more, for the former things have passed away.

REVELATION 21:4

After restlessness comes rest, peace, joy — if we be worthy.

28. Defending the Practice of Celibacy for Catholic Clergy

Newman defended priestly celibacy. He argued that it does not lead men to impurity any more than marriage keeps married ministers from impurity.

When, then, we come to the matter of fact, whether celibacy *has been* and *is*, in comparison of the marriage vow, so dangerous to a clerical body, I answer that I am very skeptical indeed that in matter of fact a married clergy *is* adorned, in any special and singular way, with the grace of purity; and this is just the very thing which Protestants take for granted....

But if matrimony does not prevent cases of immorality among Protestant ministers, it is not celibacy which causes them among Catholic priests. It is not what the Catholic Church imposes, but what human nature prompts, which leads any portion of her ecclesiastics into sin. Human nature will break out, like some wild and raging element, under any system; it bursts out under the Protestant system; it bursts out under the Catholic; passion will carry away the married clergyman as well as the unmarried priest.

Prepos, 134, 136

- Do I recognize that celibate men are no more prone to sin than those who are married?
- Jesus was celibate, as were St. John and St. Paul, and many other saints. God calls some people to celibacy and gives them the grace to live according to this calling.
- Do I pray that priests will be faithful?

JUST IMAGINE

"And there are eunuchs who have made themselves eunuchs for the sake of the kingdom of heaven. He who is able to receive this, let him receive it."

MATTHEW 19:12

REMEMBER

Human nature will break out, like some wild and raging element, under any system.

29. Power of Prayer

There are things the mind, unaided, cannot comprehend.
Understanding can come only through prayer.

I was rejoiced to be told by you that you recognized
the truth of the power of prayer. Nothing else will
clear our religious difficulties.

LD, 27:267

THINK ABOUT IT

- Do I ask God to help me overcome religious
  difficulties?
- Do I pray often? Do I pray in times of trouble?
- Ask the Holy Spirit for the gifts of wisdom,
  understanding, and science.

JUST IMAGINE

"Ask, and it will be given you; seek, and you will
find; knock, and it will be opened to you. For every
one who asks receives, and he who seeks finds, and
to him who knocks it will be opened."

MATTHEW 7:7-8

REMEMBER

Nothing but prayer will clear my religious difficulties.

God has entrusted each of us to a guardian angel, created for our care. Newman had a childlike trust in his angel and wrote of him as a friend.

My oldest friend, mine from the hour
    When first I drew my breath;
My faithful friend, that shall be mine,
    Unfailing, till my death;

Thou hast been ever at my side....

And mine, O Brother of my soul,
    When my release shall come;
Thy gentle arms shall lift me then,
    Thy wings shall waft me home.

VV, 300

THINK ABOUT IT

- God has created a brilliant and strong companion to care for me.
- I must get to know my guardian angel.
- Do I thank God for the guide and protector that he has given to me?

JUST IMAGINE

[Jesus said:] "See that you do not despise one of these little ones; for I tell you that in heaven their angels always behold the face of my Father who is in heaven."

MATTHEW 18:10

REMEMBER

My angel, my oldest friend, you have been ever at my side.

As a convert to Catholicism, Newman knew well that many non-Catholics misunderstood Mary's role in the life and work of Jesus. He wanted to correct their impressions.

There is no part of the history of Jesus but Mary has her part in it. There are those who profess to be His servants, who think that her work was ended when she bore Him, and after that she had nothing to do but disappear and be forgotten. But we, O Lord, Thy children of the Catholic Church, do not so think of Thy Mother. She brought the tender infant into the Temple, she lifted Him up in her arms when the wise men came to adore Him. She fled with Him to Egypt, she took Him up to Jerusalem when He was twelve years old. He lived with her at Nazareth for thirty years. She was with Him at the marriage-feast. Even when He had left her to preach, she hovered about Him. And now she shows herself as He toils along the Sacred Way with His cross on His shoulders. Sweet Mother, let us ever think of thee when we think of Jesus, and when we pray to Him, ever aid us by thy powerful intercession.

MD, 159

- Mary stood by her Son throughout his earthly life. She has not left him since.
- She wants to help me to be Jesus' disciple and friend.
- A mother's work does not end with childbirth; it is lifelong work. Do I consider that Mary's maternal care for us continues today?

Then [Jesus] said to the disciple, "Behold, your mother!" And from that hour the disciple took her to his own home.

JOHN 19:27

Children of the Church do not believe that Mary's work was ended when she bore Jesus.

As an old man, Cardinal Newman advised even schoolchildren to pray the Rosary in a meditative way.

And so in His mercy [God] has given us a revelation of Himself by coming amongst us, to be one of ourselves, with all the relations and qualities of humanity, to gain us over. He came down from Heaven and dwelt amongst us, and died for us. All these things are in the Creed, which contains the chief things that He has revealed to us about Himself.

Now the great power of the Rosary lies in this, that it makes the Creed into a prayer; of course, the Creed is in some sense a prayer and a great act of homage to God; but the Rosary gives us the great truths of His life and death to meditate upon, and brings them nearer to our hearts.

Sayings, 44-46

THINK ABOUT IT

- Do I realize that the Rosary is a summary and profession of my beliefs about God?
- I will try to be attentive to the scenes, the "mysteries," when I pray the Rosary.
- I will truly meditate when I pray the Rosary, so that I enter into the life and heart of Christ.

[St. Paul said:] When I came to you, brethren, I did not come proclaiming to you the testimony of God in lofty words or wisdom. For I decided to know nothing among you except Jesus Christ and him crucified.

1 CORINTHIANS 2:1-2

The Rosary makes the Creed into a prayer.

33. Make the Holy Family Your Home

As Newman urged students to make the Rosary their Creed, he counseled them to find a home with Jesus' family.

[Y]ou ought to have in the Holy Family a home with a holiness and sweetness about it that cannot be found elsewhere. This is, my dear boys, what I most earnestly ask you. I ask you when you go out into the world, as you soon must, to make the Holy Family your home, to which you may turn from all the sorrow and care of the world and find a solace, a compensation, and a refuge.

Sayings, 45

THINK ABOUT IT

- By praying to Jesus, Mary, and Joseph, I will make the Holy Family my home.
- I will remember to turn to the Holy Family when I'm sad, frustrated, or confused.
- I will try to imagine what life was like in that house and workshop in Nazareth. I will try, in some way, to imitate that life in my home and workplace.

JUST IMAGINE

And when they had performed everything according to the law of the Lord, they returned into Galilee, to their own city, Nazareth. And the child grew and became strong, filled with wisdom; and the favor of God was upon him.

LUKE 2:39-40

REMEMBER

The Holy Family is my solace, compensation, and refuge.

Christianity doesn't work on utilitarian principles. Hardships come with the territory, and always have. While applying human means, Christians must rely on faith in God.

In this age especially, not only are Catholics confessedly behindhand in political, social, physical, and economical science (more than they need be), but it is the great reproach urged against them by men of the world that so it is. And such a state of things is but the outcome of apostolic teaching. It was said in the beginning, "Take no thought for the morrow. Woe unto those that are rich. Blessed be the poor; to the poor the gospel is preached. Thou hast hid these things from the wise and prudent. Not many wise men, not many mighty, not many noble are called. Many are called, few are chosen. Take up your cross and follow me. No man can have two masters; he who loveth father or mother more than me is not worthy of me. We walk by faith, not by sight; by faith ye are saved. This is the victory that overcometh the world, our faith. Without holiness no man can see the Lord. Our God is a consuming fire." This is a very different ethical system from that whether of Bentham or of Paley.

LD, 27:388-389

THINK ABOUT IT

- In the face of difficulties, do I trust in the assistance of my Father God?
- Do I accept the lack of material means and suffering for the sake of greater goods?
- Holiness is the only true and lasting success.

JUST IMAGINE

So we are always of good courage ... for we walk by faith, not by sight.

2 CORINTHIANS 5:6-7

REMEMBER

It was said in the beginning, "Take no thought for the morrow. Woe unto those that are rich. Blessed be the poor; to the poor the gospel is preached."

35. The Church's Supernatural Origin

The Church is a divine institution — not merely human. We should keep this in mind when judging its work and attributes and teaching.

Herein is the strength of the Church…. She professes to be built upon facts, not opinions; on objective truths, not on variable sentiments; on immemorial testimony, not on private judgment; on convictions or perceptions, not on conclusions. None else but she can make this profession. She makes high claims against the temporal power, but she has that within her which justifies her. She merely acts out what she says she is. She does no more than she reasonably should do. If God has given her a specific work, no wonder she is not under the superintendence of the civil magistrate in doing it…. She is the organ and oracle, and nothing else, of a supernatural doctrine, which is independent of individuals, given to her once for all, coming down from the first ages.

Diff, I, 216-217

THINK ABOUT IT

■ Do I realize that the Church's teachings are based on truths, not sentiments or personal opinions?
■ Do I understand why the Church's doctrine cannot depend on civil laws or social opinions?

■ God has entrusted the Church with the mission of being the pillar of truth.

If I am delayed, you may know how one ought to behave in the household of God, which is the church of the living God, the pillar and bulwark of the truth.
1 TIMOTHY 3:15

The Church is the organ and oracle of a supernatural doctrine, which is independent of individuals.

36. God's Oracle

In his youth, Newman considered the pope to be the Anti-Christ. In his maturity, he came to know him as God's oracle.

I say there is only one Oracle of God, the Holy Catholic Church and the Pope as her head. To her teaching I have ever desired all my thoughts, all my words to be conformed.

Diff, II, 346

THINK ABOUT IT

- Do I read and know the *Catechism of the Catholic Church*?
- Have I read some of the encyclicals and other teachings of the popes?
- I should try to conform my life to the teachings of the Church.

JUST IMAGINE

"And I tell you, you are Peter, and on this rock I will build my church, and the powers of death shall not prevail against it."

MATTHEW 16:18

REMEMBER

There is only one Oracle of God, the Holy Catholic Church and the pope as her head.

37. The Heart's Reasons

Blaise Pascal proposed that the heart has reasons that reason cannot know. Newman agreed, in his way.

Religious persons are sometimes taunted with having only what is called an hereditary religion; with believing what they believe, and practicing what they practice, because they have been taught so to do, without any reasons of their own. Now it may very possibly happen that they have no reasons to produce, that they do not know their own reasons, that they have never analyzed what passes through their minds, and causes their impressions and convictions; but that is no proof that they have no reasons; and in truth they have always, whether they recognize them or not, very good reasons.

It does not make a man more religious that he knows why and how he became so; many a man, doubtless, was converted by the Apostles' miracles, who could not draw out accurately into words the process through which his thoughts went, and who, had he tried so to do, would have done himself injustice, and exposed himself to the criticism of the practiced disputant.

SD, 343-344

- Do I trust in the Church's teachings even when I fail to understand them fully?
- Faith is first of all faith in a person: Jesus Christ.
- I should ask Our Lord to increase my faith.

Immediately the father of the child cried out and said, "I believe; help my unbelief!"

MARK 9:24

We always have very good reasons, whether we recognize them or not.

38. Bringing Friends to Christ and the Church

Every Christian is responsible for helping the Church to grow. Newman encouraged Mrs. Wilberforce, wife of his good friend Henry, to be received into the Church and tried to allay her fears.

I don't like to leave you in your pain, which is my only reason for wishing you to be received sooner than you say.... Meanwhile do not trouble yourself over much about your confession. God asks what you can do and nothing more. Let your one thought be about His tender mercy and love for you. Say every day a prayer to each of the Five Wounds — before the Crucifix if you have one.... I consider you now a Catechumen, desirous to be received into the bosom of your tender and good Mother, as early as you can. Comfort yourself. Do not let Satan annoy you, which he will try to do. You are always in my thoughts. We will not forget you.

LD, 475-476

THINK ABOUT IT

- Do I realize that the Church is God's family on earth and that it grows like a very large tree with many branches?
- Have I brought a friend to be a member of the Catholic Church?

- I should also work for the conversion of fallen-away Catholics, especially those who are friends.

[Jesus] said therefore, "What is the kingdom of God like? And to what shall I compare it? It is like a grain of mustard seed which a man took and sowed in his garden; and it grew and became a tree, and the birds of the air made nests in its branches."

Luke 13:18-19

REMEMBER

God asks what I can do and nothing more.

39. Only the Finest for God

Newman built several churches, fitting them with stained glass and fine liturgical objects. His sister Jemima made an altar cloth for the first church he built. Newman told his sister of the reaction of the women and of Reverend Bloxam, his curate.

It looks beautiful, and B is quite in ecstasies about it. As to Mrs. Barnes she dreamed of it of a night [*sic*] at first from astonishment at its elaborateness — and Eliza B. and several others, who are work women, look at it with amazement. Rogers, taking another view of it, is equally full of admiration. Indeed we are all so happy that one is afraid of being too happy.

LD, 7:312

THINK ABOUT IT

- When it comes to decorating our churches, we should choose the best we can afford — in flowers, linens, candles, art, and music.
- What does this attitude suggest about the way I dress and groom myself for Mass?
- How may I help to beautify my parish church?

JUST IMAGINE

A woman came with an alabaster jar of ointment of pure nard, very costly, and she broke the jar and poured it over his head. But there were some who said to themselves indignantly, "Why was the ointment thus wasted? For this ointment might have been sold for more than three hundred denarii, and given to the poor." And they reproached her. But Jesus said, "Let her alone; why do you trouble her? She has done a beautiful thing to me."

MARK 14:3-6

REMEMBER

Let the things we give to God inspire astonishment and amazement.

40. Jesus Had a Home

When God became man, he sanctified our lives: our work, our family lives, our homes.

To come home again! In that word "home" how much is included.... The home life — the idea of home — is consecrated to us.... We have even a great example in our Lord Himself; for though in His public ministry He had not where to lay His head, yet we know that for the first thirty years of His life He had a home, and He therefore consecrated, in a special way, the life of home.

Addresses, 103-104

THINK ABOUT IT

- Consider how Joseph and Mary cared for Jesus and taught him.
- Think of Jesus' obedience and respect for his parents.
- Look to the home of Nazareth as an example and inspiration for your family life.

JUST IMAGINE

And he went down with them and came to Nazareth, and was obedient to them; and his mother kept all these things in her heart.

Luke 2:51

For the first thirty years of his life, Jesus had a home, and he therefore consecrated, in a special way, the life of home.

Gratitude is an important virtue. It keeps us focused on the positive things, on God's blessings. As a child of God, a Christian should give thanks many times a day.

Let us then view God's providences towards us more religiously than we have hitherto done.... Let us humbly and reverently attempt to trace His guiding hand in the years which we have hitherto lived. Let us thankfully commemorate the many mercies He has vouchsafed to us in time past, the many sins He has not remembered, the many dangers He has averted, the many prayers He has answered, the many mistakes He has corrected, the many warnings, the many lessons, the much light, the abounding comfort which He has from time to time given. Let us dwell upon times and seasons, times of trouble, times of joy, times of trial, times of refreshment. How did He cherish us as children! How did He guide us in that dangerous time when the mind began to think for itself, and the heart to open to the world! How did He with His sweet discipline restrain our passions, mortify our hopes, calm our fears, enliven our heavinesses, sweeten our desolateness, and strengthen our infirmities! ... He has been all things to us.

PPS, 5:84

- Do I thank God every day for his blessings?
- Do I see that God corrects me and guides me as a son or daughter?
- Begin each day with a short prayer of thanksgiving, and offer to God your work, concerns, and joys.

Have no anxiety about anything, but in everything by prayer and supplication with thanksgiving let your requests be made known to God. And the peace of God, which passes all understanding, will keep your hearts and your minds in Christ Jesus.

PHILIPPIANS 4:6-7

How did God cherish us as children! How did he guide us in that dangerous time when the mind began to think for itself, and the heart to open to the world!

42. Think of the Martyrs

Christians should consider how little their problems are in comparison to those borne by the apostles and martyrs. Newman found comfort in this thought.

I myself thirty or forty years ago found it impossible to stem the current of popular feeling, which was adverse to me, and found that patience and waiting was all that was left for me; but what a trifle of a difficulty was this, compared with ... three centuries ago, [when] the weapons of controversy were of a deadly character ... the rack, the gibbet, and the axe.

Addresses, 136-137

THINK ABOUT IT

- Do I read the lives of the saints?
- Am I prone to self-pity?
- I should not let the thought of my problems outweigh my gratitude to God. I have received many blessings.

JUST IMAGINE

"Rejoice over her, O heaven,
O saints and apostles and prophets,
for God has given judgment for you
    against her!
... And in her was found the blood of
    prophets and of saints,

and of all who have been slain on earth."

REVELATION 18:20, 24

REMEMBER

What a trifle my difficulties are, compared with others'.

Some Catholics limit themselves to a few vocal prayers. The saints, however, urge us to pray without ceasing. Newman practiced habitual prayer and kept regular times for meditation.

There are two modes of praying mentioned in Scripture; the one is prayer at set times and places, and in set forms; the other is what the text speaks of — continual or habitual prayer. The former of these is what is commonly called prayer, whether it be public or private. The other kind of praying may also be called holding communion with God, or living in God's sight, and this may be done all through the day, wherever we are, and is commanded us as the duty, or rather the characteristic, of those who are really servants and friends of Jesus Christ.

PPS, 7:204

THINK ABOUT IT

- Do I have a set time to say prayers to God?
- Am I aware that my relationship with God requires daily prayer?
- Do I try to live in the presence of God by raising my mind to him throughout the day?

Pray at all times in the Spirit, with all prayer and supplication. To that end keep alert with all perseverance, making supplication for all the saints.

EPHESIANS 6:18

The other kind of praying may also be called holding communion with God, or living in God's sight, and this may be done all through the day.

Many prejudices against Catholicism are overcome with charity and facts. Catholics must study in order to explain and defend the faith.

Questions may be multiplied without limit, which occur in conversation between friends in social intercourse, or in the business of life, where no argument is needed, no subtle and delicate disquisition, but a few direct words stating the fact. Half the controversies which go on in the world arise from ignorance of the facts of the case; half the prejudices against Catholicity lie in the misinformation of the prejudiced parties. Candid persons are set right, and enemies silenced, by the mere statement of what it is that we believe. It will not answer the purpose for a Catholic to say, "I leave it to theologians," "I will ask my priest"; but it will commonly give him a triumph, as easy as it is complete, if he can then and there lay down the law. I say "lay down the law"; for remarkable it is, that even those who speak against Catholicism like to hear about it, and will excuse its advocate from alleging arguments, if he can gratify their curiosity by giving them information.

Rambler, 240

- Do I realize that many prejudices against the faith are due to ignorance?
- Do I look for the right answers to the difficulties posed by friends?
- All Christians should be prepared to give answers to anyone who asks for the reason for their beliefs.

JUST IMAGINE

Always be prepared to make a defense to any one who calls you to account for the hope that is in you, yet do it with gentleness and reverence.

1 PETER 3:15

REMEMBER

Candid people are set right, and enemies silenced, by the mere statement of what it is that we believe.

45. Scripture Is Sacred

Christians must read and study Scripture if they wish to know God and to follow his commandments. Newman insisted on this while warning of the misuse of Scripture. He insisted that Scripture be understood in light of the Church's teaching and Tradition.

Scripture is a refuge in any trouble; only let us be on our guard against seeming to use it further than is fitting, or doing more than sheltering ourselves under its shadow. Let us use it according to our measure. It is far higher and wider than our need; and its language veils our feelings while it gives expression to them. It is sacred and heavenly; and it restrains and purifies, while it sanctions them.

SD, 408

THINK ABOUT IT

- Do I read sacred Scripture at least a few times a week to discover God's will, find comfort, and grow in strength?
- Do I consider that sacred Scripture is inspired by God to teach and correct his children?
- Scripture must be interpreted in keeping with the Tradition and teaching of the Church.

First of all you must understand this, that no prophecy of scripture is a matter of one's own interpretation.

2 PETER 1:20

Scripture is sacred and heavenly; and it restrains and purifies our feelings.

46. What Are You Looking For?

In everyday life, God manifests himself to his children. A Christian should therefore look for God in the ordinary events of the day.

This is the very definition of a Christian — one who looks for Christ; not who looks for gain, or distinction, or power, or pleasure, or comfort, but who looks "for the Savior, the Lord Jesus Christ." This, according to Scripture, is the essential mark, this is the foundation of a Christian, from which every thing else follows.

SD, 278-279

THINK ABOUT IT

- Do you think about Jesus throughout the day?
- Do you think of how to please him?
- A child of God seeks his Father God in all the events of the day.

JUST IMAGINE

"Afterward the other maidens came also, saying, 'Lord, lord, open to us.' But he replied, 'Truly, I say to you, I do not know you.' Watch therefore, for you know neither the day nor the hour."

MATTHEW 25:11-13

REMEMBER

This is the very definition of a Christian: one who looks for Christ.

47. Joy, the Sign of a Christian

Joy is one of the fruits the Holy Spirit gives to souls. At the funeral of one of his friends, Newman spoke of the Christian joy that had been manifest in the man's life.

This, then, is the third chief grace of primitive Christianity — joy in all its forms; not only a pure heart, not only a clean hand, but, thirdly, a cheerful countenance. I say joy in all its forms, for in true joyfulness many graces are included; joyful people are loving; joyful people are forgiving; joyful people are munificent. Joy, if it be Christian joy, the refined joy of the mortified and persecuted, makes men peaceful, serene, thankful, gentle, affectionate, sweet-tempered, pleasant, hopeful; it is graceful, tender, touching, winning. All this were the Christians of the New Testament, for they had obtained what they desired. They had desired to sacrifice the kingdom of the world and all its pomps for the love of Christ, whom they had seen, whom they loved, in whom they believed, in whom they delighted.

SD, 286-287

THINK ABOUT IT

■ Do I have joy in my life, a joy rooted in my relationship with God?

■ Do I transmit Christian joy to those around me?

■ Christian joy goes hand in hand with suffering, at times due to injustice and even persecution.

JUST IMAGINE

"Blessed are you when men hate you, and when they exclude you and revile you, and cast out your name as evil, on account of the Son of man! Rejoice in that day, and leap for joy, for behold, your reward is great in heaven; for so their fathers did to the prophets."

LUKE 6:22-23

REMEMBER

Joy, if it be Christian joy, the refined joy of the mortified and persecuted, makes us peaceful, serene, thankful.

What is life for the multitude who do not live for God?

Man is not sufficient for his own happiness; he is not happy except the Presence of God be with him. When he was created, God breathed into him that supernatural life of the Spirit which is his true happiness: and when he fell, he lost the divine gift, and with it his happiness also. Ever since he has been unhappy; ever since he has a void within him which needs filling, and he knows not how to fill it. He scarcely realizes his own need: only his actions show that he feels it, for he is ever restless when he is not dull and insensible, seeking in one thing or another that blessing which he has lost. Multitudes, indeed, there are, whose minds have never been opened; and multitudes who stupefy and deaden their minds, till they lose their natural hunger and thirst: but, whether aware of their need or not, whether made restless by it or not, still all men have it, and the Gospel supplies it.

SD, 312

THINK ABOUT IT

- How can I help others to be happier, knowing the presence of God?
- Do my friends understand the difference grace makes in someone's life?

■ Do I allow corners of my life to remain sad, without the light of the Spirit?

You must no longer live as the Gentiles do, in the futility of their minds; they are darkened in their understanding, alienated from the life of God because of the ignorance that is in them, due to their hardness of heart; they have become callous and have given themselves up to licentiousness, greedy to practice every kind of uncleanness. ... Be renewed in the spirit of your minds, and put on the new nature, created after the likeness of God in true righteousness and holiness.

EPHESIANS 4:17-19, 23-24

Those without God are restless when they are not insensible, seeking in one thing or another that blessing which they have lost.

49. Speak Kindly

Newman strove never to speak about others' defects.

Accordingly, as persons have deep feelings, so they will find the necessity of self-control, lest they should say what they ought not.

SD, 299-300

THINK ABOUT IT

- Do I refrain from speaking of others' defects or sins unnecessarily?
- Do I make an effort to avoid revealing confidences?
- The practice of prudence entails knowing when and how to say something.

JUST IMAGINE

If any one thinks he is religious, and does not bridle his tongue but deceives his heart, this man's religion is vain.

James 1:26

REMEMBER

Accordingly, as people have deep feelings, so they will find the necessity of self-control.

50. Actions Speak Louder Than Words

The Gospel is to be lived, not only spoken about. Christ urges us to imitate him; and in the measure that we do, others will come to know and love him better.

Moreover, meekness, gentleness, patience, and love, have in themselves a strong power to melt the heart of those who witness them. Cheerful suffering, too, leads spectators to sympathy, till, perhaps, a reaction takes place in the minds of men, and they are converted by the sight, and glorify their Father which is in heaven.

SD, 304-305

THINK ABOUT IT

- Are my actions in keeping with my words and principles?
- Do I demand of others what I fail to do myself?
- People are convinced when they see that my example corresponds to my words.

JUST IMAGINE

"Let your light so shine before men, that they may see your good works and give glory to your Father who is in heaven."

MATTHEW 5:16

Meekness, gentleness, patience, and love have in themselves a strong power to melt the heart of those who witness them.

51. Lasting Peace in Heaven

Amid the struggles and trials of daily life, the Christian finds comfort in the thought of heaven.

May He, as of old, choose "the foolish things of the world to confound the wise, and the weak things of the world to confound the things which are mighty"! May He support us all the day long, till the shades lengthen, and the evening comes, and the busy world is hushed, and the fever of life is over, and our work is done! Then in His mercy may He give us safe lodging, and a holy rest, and peace at the last!

SD, 307

THINK ABOUT IT

- Life is short; eternity is forever.
- Do I try to measure the importance of things with the perspective of eternal life?
- A Christian should think of communion with God in heaven and desire it.

JUST IMAGINE

"For what does it profit a man, to gain the whole world and forfeit his life?"

Mark 8:36

REMEMBER

May God support us all the day long, till the shades lengthen, and the evening comes, and the busy world is hushed.

52. The Holy Eucharist Is a Feast

The Holy Mass is a sacrifice, but it is also a divine banquet where Christ becomes our nourishment. While still an Anglican, Newman wrote the following.

To rejoice, then, and to keep festival, is a Christian duty, under all circumstances. Indeed, is not this plain, by considering the obligation, yet the nature, of that chief Gospel Ordinance which we celebrate today? There is an ordinance which we are bound to observe always till the Lord come: is it an ordinance of humiliation and self-abasement, or is it a feast? The Holy Eucharist is a Feast; we cannot help feasting, we cannot elude our destiny of joy and thanksgiving, if we would be Christians.

SD, 388-389

THINK ABOUT IT

- Do I prepare for Holy Mass as much as I would for a special banquet?
- Do I prepare my soul through prayer and the Sacrament of Penance?
- How do I care for my outward appearance as I approach this holy feast?

JUST IMAGINE

"But when the king came in to look at the guests, he saw there a man who had no wedding garment;

and he said to him, 'Friend, how did you get in here without a wedding garment?' And he was speechless."

MATTHEW 22:11-12

The Holy Eucharist is a Feast; we cannot help feasting, we cannot elude our destiny of joy and thanksgiving, if we would be Christians.

53. Know Yourself

Newman examined his conscience daily for sins and imperfections and to seek God's forgiveness.

Think nothing preferable to a knowledge of yourselves, true repentance, a resolve to live to God, to die to the world, deep humility, hatred of sin, and of yourselves as you are sinners, a clear and habitual view of the coming judgment.

SD, 394

THINK ABOUT IT

- Am I convinced that I am a sinner in constant need of God's forgiveness and mercy?
- Do I realize the need to examine my conscience at a set time each night?
- I should hate sin because it offends God and separates me from him.

JUST IMAGINE

"But the tax collector, standing far off, would not even lift up his eyes to heaven, but beat his breast, saying, 'God, be merciful to me a sinner!' "

Luke 18:13

REMEMBER

Think nothing preferable to a knowledge of ourselves, true repentance, a resolve to live to God.

54. Turning Away From God

Many have an excessively optimistic view of human goodness. There is a generalized forgetfulness of sin.

The one peculiar and characteristic sin of the world is this, that whereas God would have us live for the life to come, the world would make us live for this life. This, I say, is the world's sin; it lives for this life, not for the next. It takes, as the main scope of human exertion, an end which God forbids; and consequently all that it does becomes evil, because directed to a wrong end.

SD, 80-81

THINK ABOUT IT

- What motives habitually guide my behavior?
- What earthly "reward" do I seek: the praise of others, comfort, sensual pleasure … ?
- How can I turn from earthly rewards so as to gain my heavenly reward?

JUST IMAGINE

All have sinned and fall short of the glory of God.

ROMANS 3:23

REMEMBER

God would have us live for the life to come.

God calls us to make holy our everyday circumstances: family life and work. Newman described this a century before the Second Vatican Council would solemnly proclaim it.

In all things, then, we must spiritualize this world; and if you ask for instances how to do this, I give you the following. When a nation enters Christ's Church, and takes her yoke upon its shoulder, then it formally joins itself to the cause of God, and separates itself from the evil world. When the civil magistrate defends the Christian faith, and sets it up in all honor in high places, as a beacon to the world, so far he gives himself to God, and sanctifies and spiritualizes that portion of it over which he has power. When men put aside a portion of their gains for God's service, then they sanctify those gains. When the head of a household observes family prayer and other religious offices, and shows that, like Abraham, he is determined with God's help to honor Him, then he joins himself to the kingdom of God, and rescues his household from its natural relationship with this unprofitable world. When a man hallows in his private conduct holy seasons, this is offering up of God's gifts to God, and sanctifying all seasons by the sacrifice of some. When a man who is rich, and whose duty calls on him to be hospitable, is careful also to feed the hungry and clothe the naked, thus he sanctifies his riches. When he is in the midst of plenty, and observes self-denial; when he builds his house, but builds Churches too; when he plants and sows, but pays tithes; when he buys and sells, but withal gives largely to religion....

SD, 109-110

THINK ABOUT IT

- Christians sanctify the world when they take the love of Christ to their homes and to their workplaces.
- Would people guess from my actions that I believe in Jesus Christ?
- Do I seek opportunities to serve others and to show kindness to everyone, even those who annoy me?

JUST IMAGINE

"Then the King will say to those at his right hand, 'Come, O blessed of my Father, inherit the kingdom prepared for you from the foundation of the world; for I was hungry and you gave me food, I was thirsty and you gave me drink, I was a stranger and you welcomed me, I was naked and you clothed me, I was sick and you visited me, I was in prison and you came to me.'"

MATTHEW 25:34-36

REMEMBER

In all things, we must spiritualize this world.

56. Don't Write Anyone Off

Newman knew how to forgive others. In dealing with opponents, he practiced Christ's charity and mercy.

There is no man ever so bad but to our erring eyes has some redeeming points of character. There is no man but has some human feelings or other: and those very feelings impress us with a sort of conviction that he cannot possibly be the destined companion of evil spirits. Hell is the habitation of no human affections. Let a man be ever so blood-stained, so awfully blasphemous, or so profligate, yet at least, at times, perhaps when in pain or weariness, he shows something to excite our interest and pity. And if not, then his very pain seems to plead for him.

SD, 75

THINK ABOUT IT

- Are there people I do not love or wish to reach for Christ?
- I should consider the lack of affection for people as a triumph for hell.
- I must search out the good in others.

"And whenever you stand praying, forgive, if you have anything against any one; so that your Father also who is in heaven may forgive you your trespasses."

MARK 11:25

Hell is the habitation of no human affections.

57. Restoring God's Image

Jesus Christ is the perfect image of the Father. He restores in us the image that was damaged by sin.

Christ came to make a new world. He came into the world to regenerate it in Himself, to make a new beginning, to be the beginning of the creation of God, to gather together in one, and recapitulate all things in Himself. The rays of His glory were scattered through the world; one state of life had some of them, another others. The world was like some fair mirror, broken in pieces, and giving back no one uniform image of its Maker. But He came to combine what was dissipated, to recast what was shattered in Himself. He began all excellence, and of His fullness have all we received.

SD, 61

THINK ABOUT IT

- Do you remember that you are the image of God?
- When you see your faults and those of others, consider the comparison with a broken mirror.
- Try to let Christ's light shine through your words and actions.

[Christ] is the image of the invisible God, the first-born of all creation.

COLOSSIANS 1:15

For those whom [God] foreknew he also predestined to be conformed to the image of his Son, in order that he might be the first-born among many brethren.

ROMANS 8:29

REMEMBER

Jesus came to combine what was dissipated, to recast what was shattered in himself.

58. Bear Witness to Christ

Christ sent his disciples to bear witness to the truth; they were to be a light for the world. Each Christian is a disciple of Christ, also called to be an ambassador for Christ.

This is the glory of the Church, to speak, to do, and to suffer, with that grace which Christ brought and diffused abroad.... Not the few and the conspicuous alone, but all her children, high and low, who walk worthy of her and her Divine Lord, will be shadows of Him. All of us are bound, according to our opportunities — first to learn the truth; and moreover, we must not only know, but we must impart our knowledge. Nor only so, but next we must bear witness to the truth.

SD, 62

THINK ABOUT IT

- Christian holiness and witness are an obligation and a privilege for each one of God's children, not only a few.
- Am I a daily witness of God's love to my family members and co-workers?
- To be a better witness for God, I need to grow in knowledge and love.

"You are the light of the world. A city set on a hill cannot be hid."

MATTHEW 5:14

Not the few and the conspicuous alone, but all the Church's children, high and low, who walk worthy of her and her Divine Lord, will be shadows of him.

Newman endured the slander, envy, and scorn of many, first as an Anglican because of his Catholic principles, and later a Catholic because of suspicion of his Anglican past. He learned to accept this as part of the cross.

My brethren, so many of you as are sensitive of the laughter or contempt of the world, this is your cross; you must wear it, you must endure it patiently; it is the mark of your conformity to Christ; He despised the shame: you must learn to endure it, from the example and by the aid of your Savior. You must love the praise of God more than the praise of men. It is the very trial suited to you, appointed for you, to establish you in the faith. You are not tempted with gain or ambition, but with ridicule. And be sure, that unless you withstand it, you cannot endure hardships as good soldiers of Jesus Christ, you will not endure other temptations which are to follow.

PPS, 7:46-47

THINK ABOUT IT

- Do I accept that to be a disciple of Christ I will sometimes meet with mockery and injustice?
- Do I look to Jesus' example of patient endurance during his Passion?

- I should seek God's glory and praise, not the shallow and passing praise of this world.

Then Jesus told his disciples, "If any man would come after me, let him deny himself and take up his cross and follow me."

MATTHEW 16:24

We must love the praise of God more than the praise of men.

60. The Gospel Paradox

The Gospel paradox is that suffering becomes a source of blessing, persecution a source of joy. Newman urged Christians not to shrink from the cross but to embrace it.

Meanwhile, whether we will believe it or no, the truth remains, that the strength of the Church, as heretofore, does not lie in earthly law, or human countenance, or civil station, but in her proper gifts; in those great gifts which our Lord pronounced to be beatitudes. Blessed are the poor in spirit, the mourners, the meek, the thirsters after righteousness, the merciful, the pure in heart, the peacemakers, the persecuted.

SD, 274

THINK ABOUT IT

- Do I rebel when God does not grant what I pray for?
- Do I rely on God's grace to face daily difficulties and hardships?
- I need to remember that the growth of the Church depends foremost on prayer and God's graces.

[Jesus said:] "Blessed are you when men revile you and persecute you and utter all kinds of evil against you falsely on my account. Rejoice and be glad, for your reward is great in heaven, for so men persecuted the prophets who were before you."

MATTHEW 5:11-12

REMEMBER

The strength of the Church does not lie in her status, but in her proper gifts.

61. A Child's Happiness

Jesus teaches us to live like little children before God.
A child of God depends on his Father for everything
and finds happiness in him.

O happy soul, who hast loved neither the world nor the things of the world apart from God! Happy soul, who, amid the world's toil, hast chosen the one thing needful, that better part which can never be taken away! Happy soul, who, being the counselor and guide, the stay, the light and joy, the benefactor of so many, yet hast ever depended simply, as a little child, on the grace of thy God and the merits and strength of thy Redeemer!

OS, 279-280

THINK ABOUT IT

- Do I seek my strength in God?
- Amid my daily occupations do I give priority to times for conversation with God?
- I should have a more keen awareness that before God I am a little child.

JUST IMAGINE

[Jesus said:] "Truly, I say to you, unless you turn and become like children, you will never enter the kingdom of heaven."

MATTHEW 18:3

Depend simply, as a child, on the grace of God and the merits and strength of our Redeemer.

62. The Hunger for True Bread

Though always busy, Newman gave priority to daily Mass. As an old man, he continued to celebrate Mass. He drew strength from the Eucharist and offered Mass for the souls of deceased friends.

The poor, those multitudes who pass their days in constrained suffering, they, by the stern persuasion of that suffering, are looking out for Him. But we, my Brethren, who are in easy circumstances, or in a whirl of business, or in a labyrinth of cares, or in a war of passions, or in the race of wealth, or honor, or station, or in the pursuits of science or of literature, alas! we are the very men who are likely to have no regard, no hunger or thirst, no relish for the true bread of heaven and the living water.

OS, 45-46

THINK ABOUT IT

- Do I look forward to attending Mass, when possible even on weekdays?
- Am I giving undue importance to material things that cannot satisfy the human heart's desire for happiness?
- A good way to prepare for Mass is to tell God that I wish to receive him in the Holy Eucharist.

"Do not labor for the food which perishes, but for the food which endures to eternal life, which the Son of man will give to you; for on him has God the Father set his seal."

JOHN 6:27

I want to regard, hunger and thirst for, and relish the true bread of heaven and the living water.

Materialism is an illness that chokes the spiritual life. Men make gods of their material possessions, their belly, or sensual pleasures.

One man determines to rise in life, another is wrapt up in his family. Numbers get through the day and the year with the alternation of routine business and holyday recreation. Rich men are lavish in pomp and show; poor men give themselves to intemperance; the young give themselves up to sensual pleasures. They cannot live without an object of life, though it be an object unworthy of an immortal spirit.

Is it wonderful then, that, when the True Life, the very supply of the need of mankind, was again offered them in its fullness, that it should have carried power with it to persuade them to accept it?

OS, 52-53

THINK ABOUT IT

- Do I let material cares or sensual pleasures rule me?
- Am I looking for what is true and noble?
- God has made us with an immortal soul that longs for what is lasting.

"The thief comes only to steal and kill and destroy; I came that they may have life, and have it abundantly."

JOHN 10:10

We cannot live without an object of life. May it be an object worthy of an immortal spirit.

64. Build on a Solid Foundation

From his youth at Oxford, Newman sought Christ in daily prayer and tried to order his life according to God's commandments and the Church's teachings. When he became Catholic, the Eucharist and confession became his foundation for life.

It is not our attainments or our talents, it is not philosophy or science, letters or arts, which will make us dear to God. It is not secular favor, or civil position, which can make us worthy the attention and the interest of the true Christian…. "Unless the Lord build the House, they labor in vain that build it." Idle is our labor, worthless is our toil, ashes is our fruit, corruption is our reward, unless we begin the foundation of this great undertaking in faith and prayer, and sanctify it by purity of life.

OS, 58-59

THINK ABOUT IT

- Have I laid a strong foundation for my life?
- Do I give excessive importance to the status afforded by my work or connections?
- Meditating on God's word, we are able to lay a solid foundation of our lives.

"Every one then who hears these words of mine and does them will be like a wise man who built his house upon the rock; and the rain fell, and the floods came, and the winds blew and beat upon that house, but it did not fall, because it had been founded on the rock."

MATTHEW 7:24-25

It is not our attainments or our talents, it is not philosophy or science, letters or arts, which will make us dear to God.

65. There Are No Short Ways to Perfection

Christian holiness requires the fulfillment of one's duties for love of God. Newman was conscientious in fulfilling his obligations as a pastor and later superior of the Birmingham Oratory.

It is the saying of holy men that, if we wish to be perfect, we have nothing more to do than to perform the ordinary duties of the day well…. We must bear in mind what is meant by perfection. It does not mean any extraordinary service, anything out of the way, or especially heroic — not all have the opportunity of heroic acts, of sufferings — but it means what the word perfection ordinarily means. By perfect we mean that which has no flaw in it, that which is complete, that which is consistent, that which is sound — we mean the opposite to imperfect…. He, then, is perfect who does the work of the day perfectly, and we need not go beyond this to seek for perfection. You need not go out of the round of the day.

MD, 285-286

THINK ABOUT IT

- Do I finish my work in a responsible manner?
- Do I fulfill my daily obligations well?

■ Perfection does not consist primarily in accomplishing big things.

JUST IMAGINE

Do not be conformed to this world but be transformed by the renewal of your mind, that you may prove what is the will of God, what is good and acceptable and perfect.

ROMANS 12:2

REMEMBER

We must bear in mind what is meant by perfection. It does not mean any extraordinary service, anything out of the way, or especially heroic.

66. Learn How to Do Without

Newman loved the comfort of his home, Oriel College, a library — yet he gave up some of these comforts to serve Jesus better.

Jesus would give up everything of this world, before He left it. He exercised the most perfect poverty. When He left the Holy House of Nazareth, and went out to preach, He had not where to lay His head. He lived on the poorest food, and on what was given to Him by those who loved and served Him. And therefore He chose a death in which not even His clothes were left to Him. He parted with what seemed most necessary, and even a part of Him, by the law of human nature since the fall. Grant us in like manner, O dear Lord, to care nothing for anything on earth, and to bear the loss of all things, and to endure even shame, reproach, contempt, and mockery, rather than that Thou shalt be ashamed of us at the last day.

MD, 164

THINK ABOUT IT

■ Do I consider that Jesus voluntarily did without many material things?

■ Do I complain if I lack some items of clothing or cannot go out to a restaurant?

- In his voluntary detachment from material things, Jesus teaches us to seek first what is most important: our relationship with God.

JUST IMAGINE

And Jesus said to him, "Foxes have holes, and birds of the air have nests; but the Son of man has nowhere to lay his head."

MATTHEW 8:20

REMEMBER

Jesus exercised the most perfect poverty.

67. God Made Us Valuable to Himself

From the cross we learn all the virtues. Newman meditated on Our Lord's Passion. He composed two sets of meditations on the Stations of the Cross.

"Consummatum est." It is completed — it has come to a full end. The mystery of God's love towards us is accomplished. The price is paid, and we are redeemed. The Eternal Father determined not to pardon us without a price, in order to show us especial favor. He condescended to make us valuable to Him. What we buy we put a value on. He might have saved us without a price — by the mere *fiat* of His will. But to show His love for us He took a price, which, if there was to be a price set upon us at all, if there was any ransom at all to be taken for the guilt of our sins, could be nothing short of the death of His Son in our nature. O my God and Father, Thou hast valued us so much as to pay the highest of all possible prices for our sinful souls — and shall we not love and choose Thee above all things as the one necessary and one only good?

MD, 166

THINK ABOUT IT

■ Do I reflect on God's immense love for me in the Passion and Death of his Son?

- Do I glance at the crucifix with love, asking Jesus for the grace to correspond to his love?
- I should meditate on God's love for me by praying the Stations of the Cross.

You were bought with a price. So glorify God in your body.

1 CORINTHIANS 6:20

God condescended to make us valuable to him.

68. In Mary's Arms

The life of the Mother of God is intimately connected with the life of her Son. Newman explained this truth in his writings and urged Christians to sympathize with Mary's sufferings.

He is thy property now, O Virgin Mother, once again, for He and the world have met and parted. He went out from thee to do His Father's work — and He has done and suffered it. Satan and bad men have now no longer any claim upon Him — too long has He been in their arms. Satan took Him up aloft to the high mountain; evil men lifted Him up upon the Cross. He has not been in thy arms, O Mother of God, since He was a child — but now thou hast a claim upon Him, when the world has done its worst. For thou art the all-favored, all-blessed, all-gracious Mother of the Highest. We rejoice in this great mystery. He has been hidden in thy womb, He has lain in thy bosom, He has been suckled at thy breasts, He has been carried in thy arms — and now that He is dead, He is placed upon thy lap. Virgin Mother of God, pray for us.

MD, 167

THINK ABOUT IT

■ The Virgin Mary's life was completely bound to her Son's, including his Passion. By remaining close to her, we will be close to Jesus.

- Like Jesus, I should give myself to Mary's maternal care.
- I will imitate Mary, following Jesus wherever he leads.

When Jesus saw his mother, and the disciple whom he loved standing near, he said to his mother, "Woman, behold, your son!"

Then he said to the disciple, "Behold, your mother!" And from that hour the disciple took her to his own home.

JOHN 19:26-27

He has been carried in thy arms — and now that he is dead, he is placed upon thy lap. Virgin Mother of God, pray for us.

69. Not Worrying About What Others Think

Through much of his life, Newman worried about the regard others had for him. Then he realized that such concern was often misguided. In imitation of Christ, he embraced calumnies said about him.

Jesus, when He was nearest to His everlasting triumph, seemed to be farthest from triumphing. When He was nearest upon entering upon His kingdom, and exercising all power in heaven and earth, He was lying dead in a cave of the rock. He was wrapped round in burying-clothes, and confined within a sepulchre of stone, where He was soon to have a glorified spiritual body, which could penetrate all substances, go to and fro quicker than thought, and was about to ascend on high. Make us to trust in Thee, O Jesus, that Thou wilt display in us a similar providence. Make us sure, O Lord, that the greater is our distress, the nearer we are to Thee. The more men scorn us, the more Thou dost honor us. The more men insult over us, the higher Thou wilt exalt us. The more they forget us, the more Thou dost keep us in mind. The more they abandon us, the closer Thou wilt bring us to Thyself.

MD, 168

- How do I react when I am mistreated?
- Do I accept small slights and ingratitude with humility?
- Jesus teaches us in his suffering to accept suffering with humility.

JUST IMAGINE

"Remember the word that I said to you, 'A servant is not greater than his master.' If they persecuted me, they will persecute you; if they kept my word, they will keep yours also."

JOHN 15:20

REMEMBER

Make us sure, O Lord, that the greater is our distress, the nearer we are to you. The more men scorn us, the more you honor us.

70. Living in God's Presence

Some people think it strange or exaggerated to pray throughout the day. They have a mistaken notion of God and of man's relation to him. Newman, instead, taught parishioners that praying and living in the presence of God is natural.

A man who is religious, is religious morning, noon, and night; his religion is a certain character, a mould in which his thoughts, words, and actions are cast, all forming parts of one and the same whole. He sees God in all things; every course of action he directs towards those spiritual objects which God has revealed to him; every occurrence of the day, every event, every person met with, all news which he hears, he measures by the standard of God's will. And a person who does this may be said almost literally to pray without ceasing; for, knowing himself to be in God's presence, he is continually led to address Him reverently, whom he sets always before him, in the inward language of prayer and praise, of humble confession and joyful trust.

PPS, 7:205-206

THINK ABOUT IT

- Do I often think of God throughout the day?
- Do I ask God's guidance and remember to thank him for his blessings?

- I should speak with God about the small occurrences of each day. How can I remember to do so more often?

JUST IMAGINE

Rejoice always, pray constantly, give thanks in all circumstances; for this is the will of God in Christ Jesus for you.

1 THESSALONIANS 5:16-18

REMEMBER

Someone who is religious, is religious morning, noon, and night.

Religious knowledge does us little good if it merely makes us proud. We need to practice the faith as well. Newman was brilliant, but understood that religious knowledge is a gift from God, which anyone may humbly attain.

Do we think to become better men by knowing more? Little knowledge is required for religious obedience. The poor and rich, the learned and unlearned, are here on a level. We have all of us the means of doing our duty; we have not the *will*, and this no knowledge can give. We have need to subdue our own minds, and this no other person *can* do for us. The case is different in matters of learning and science. There others can and do labor for us; *we* can make use of *their* labors; we begin where they ended; thus things progress, and each successive age knows more than the preceding. But in religion each must begin, go on, and end, for himself. The religious history of each individual is as solitary and complete as the history of the world. Each man will, of course, gain more knowledge as he studies Scripture more, and prays and meditates more; but he cannot make another man wise or holy by his own advance in wisdom or holiness.

PPS, 7:247-248

- Do I restrain vain thoughts about my learning and accomplishments?
- Faith and obedience in religion are not the result of knowledge; they are based on humility.
- Each person advances in wisdom on his own, by means of a humble path of prayer and study.

Do nothing from selfishness or conceit, but in humility count others better than yourselves.

PHILIPPIANS 2:3

We need to subdue our own minds, and no other person can do this for us.

72. You Are in God's Hands

Newman reminded his friends to trust in God's loving Providence. He wrote the following to his godchild John Edward Bowden, who was staying in the countryside with his grandfather.

We are all in God's Hands, and He orders us about, each in his own way; happy for us, only, if we can realize this, and submit as children to a dear Father, whatever He may please to do with us. It must be a great trial to you, being out of the way of Mass and the Sacraments — but He can make up all things to you. He is with you, and Our Blessed Lady, and our dear Father Philip, and all the more, I am sure, for your separation from us, which tries us as it does you — but God is great and good.

LD, 13:261

THINK ABOUT IT

- Do I often turn to my Father God for help?
- As a child of God, do I seek to do his will in my daily tasks and projects?
- I should put aside excessive worry and instead place my concerns in God's fatherly hands.

"Your Father knows what you need before you ask him."

MATTHEW 6:8

We are all in God's hands, and he orders us about, each in his own way; happy for us, only, if we can realize this, and submit as children to a dear Father.

73. Keeping in Touch With Friends

Newman was a faithful correspondent and loved to receive letters from friends. Early in 1850, he wrote to his friend Maria Giberne, who soon after became Roman Catholic.

You have been very good in writing, and I have been joyful to receive your letters — if I have not always answered promptly, it is from my many engagements. Correspondence, alas, takes up great part of the day — and life is getting [on] — when shall I do any thing? And now I have nothing more to say except to commend you to God and His blessed Mother, and all the good Saints whom you have as your Patrons — and to pray that He in His own time would bring you home and make you blessed and a blessing wherever you are.

LD, 13:415.

THINK ABOUT IT

- Do I make time to write to friends and to reply to their questions?
- Do I pray regularly for my friends? Do I ask God for the conversion to the Catholic faith of those who are not Catholic?
- While I write to a friend I can also pray to God for him and invoke his guardian angel.

See with what large letters I am writing to you with my own hand.

GALATIANS 6:11

Peace be to you. The friends greet you. Greet the friends, every one of them.

3 JOHN 15

We should be very good in writing, and joyful to receive letters from others.

Newman told some of his close Anglican friends, who had sufficient knowledge of religious truth, that they should become Roman Catholic. He wrote to one of these, Mrs. Catherine Froude.

You must come to the Church, not to avoid [the world], but to save your soul. If this is your motive, all is right — you cannot be disappointed — but the other motive is dangerous.... You must come to learn that religion which the Apostles introduced and which was in the world long before the Reformation was dreamed of — but a religion not so easy and natural to you, or congenial, because you have been bred up in another from your youth.

LD, 12:224-225

THINK ABOUT IT

- Salvation, and nothing less, is the proper motive for a person to convert to Catholicism.
- The Catholic Church is the body established by God through the apostles as the ordinary means of salvation.
- I should help close friends to convert to the Catholic faith.

This is good, and it is acceptable in the sight of God our Savior, who desires all men to be saved and to come to the knowledge of the truth. For there is one God, and there is one mediator between God and men, the man Christ Jesus, who gave himself as a ransom for all, the testimony to which was borne at the proper time. For this I was appointed a preacher and apostle (I am telling the truth, I am not lying), a teacher of the Gentiles in faith and truth.

1 TIMOTHY 2:3-5

REMEMBER

A person must come to the Church, not to avoid the world, but to save his soul.

75. Reviving Old Friendships

Newman strove to rekindle friendships even when he and his friends disagreed on religious matters. He dedicated a book to a longtime friend who had remained Anglican.

Half a century and more has passed since you first allowed me to know you familiarly, and to possess your friendship. Now it is pleasant to me to look back upon those old Oxford days, in which we were together, and in memory of them, to dedicate to you a Volume, written for the most part, before the currents of opinion and the course of events carried friends away in different directions, and brought about great changes and bitter separations.

DA, i

THINK ABOUT IT

- Do I remember old friends and reach out to them?
- Am I able to overcome differences with friends?
- Genuine friendship endures the storms and separation of many years.

JUST IMAGINE

[Years after St. Paul parted ways with St. Mark (Acts 15:39-40) he wrote:] Aristarchus my fellow prisoner greets you, and Mark the cousin of Barnabas

(concerning whom you have received instructions —
if he comes to you, receive him).

COLOSSIANS 4:10

REMEMBER

It is pleasant to look back upon old days and dedicate
new works to friends.

76. Friendship Based on Christ

Newman had many friends and a few very close friendships. In each case, the love between Newman and his closest friends — John W. Bowden, Hurrell Froude, John Keble, Edward Pusey, Henry Wilberforce, Maria Giberne, and Ambrose St. John — was based on a deep mutual love for God.

But what is it that can bind two friends together in intimate converse for a course of years, but the participation in something that is Unchangeable and essentially Good, and what is this but religion? Religious tastes alone are unalterable. The Saints of God continue in one way, while the fashions of the world change; and a faithful and indestructible friendship may thus be a test of parties, so loving each other, having the love of God seated in their hearts.

PPS, 5:59

THINK ABOUT IT

- Do I try to love friends unselfishly for love of God?
- Do I make an effort to help friends grow in a deeper relationship with God?
- The secret for a lasting and noble friendship between people is friendship with God.

Beloved, let us love one another; for love is of God.

1 John 4:7

A faithful and indestructible friendship may thus be a test of parties, so loving each other, having the love of God seated in their hearts.

We hope these meditations with John Henry Newman have helped you to deepen your relationship with God and grow in his loving plans for you.

Newman's meditations are a rich source for prayer and for growth in Christian virtues. As you have seen, Newman speaks on perennial themes — such as faith, hope, and love for God — as well as on themes touching modern man — such as the relationship between faith and science, and the laity's call to holiness. His example of friendship and his reflections on friendship are an inspiration for people of all times.

To help the reader choose which of Newman's many books to read, we would suggest his sermons, especially the *Parochial and Plain Sermons*. In these you will find a wealth of insights into sacred Scripture and the Christian life. Next you may want to consider reading his novel about conversion and the early Christians, *Callista: A Tale of the Third Century*.

In addition to reading Newman's writings, look up to Newman, not only as a wise scholar and writer, but also as a spiritual father, a friend, and now Blessed John Henry Newman. Ask him to guide you and to intercede for you before God, in your effort to correspond more fully to the call to holiness in daily life.

MIKE AQUILINA
FR. JUAN R. VÉLEZ

MIKE AQUILINA is executive vice president of the St. Paul Center for Biblical Theology. He has written or edited more than twenty books on Catholic history, doctrine, and devotion, including the best-selling *What Catholics Believe*.

FATHER JUAN R. VÉLEZ, a former physician, wrote a doctoral dissertation in theology on the writings of John Henry Newman. He is the author of a forthcoming biography on Newman. He lives in Southern California.